CULTURE AND IRONY
Studies in Joseph Conrad's Major Novels

CULTURE AND IRONY
Studies in Joseph Conrad's Major Novels

by
Anthony Winner

UNIVERSITY PRESS OF VIRGINIA
Charlottesville

This is a title in the series

THE UNIVERSITY PRESS OF VIRGINIA
Copyright © 1988 by the Rector and Visitors
of the University of Virginia

First published 1988

Design by Janet Anderson

Library of Congress Cataloging-in-Publication Data

Winner, Anthony.
Culture and irony.
(Virginia victorian studies)
Includes index.
1. Conrad, Joseph, 1857–1924—Criticism and
interpretation. 2. Ethics in literature. 3. Irony
in literature. I. Title. II. Series.
PR6005.04Z934 1988   823'.912   87-23219
ISBN 0-8139-2946-6

Contents

	Acknowledgments	vii
	Introduction: A Choice of Ironies	1
I.	*Lord Jim:* Irony and Dream	16
II.	*Nostromo:* The Irony of Faithful Service	43
III.	*The Secret Agent:* The Irony of Home Truths	70
IV.	*Under Western Eyes:* Irony and Women's Strength	92
	Notes	127
	Index	131

Acknowledgments

I am indebted beyond formal acknowledgment to Michael Levenson and David H. Lynn for their encouragement and counsel. Students, colleagues, and friends have all helped enormously. I should like to mention in particular Richard L. Barr, Deborah M. Garfield, Hoyt N. Duggan, and Donald R. Wehrs. Corinne McCutchan has given more than generously of her time and skill as an editor and typist. A Sesquicentennial Associateship at the Center for Advanced Studies of the University of Virginia provided time for research and writing.

With the exception of several quotations from the first edition of *Nostromo*, all quotations from Conrad's work are from the Kent Edition (New York: Doubleday, Page, 1926) and are cited by page number in the text.

CULTURE AND IRONY
Studies in Joseph Conrad's Major Novels

Introduction

A Choice of Ironies

ONE MAY SAY of the ironies and ambiguities that mark Conrad's four major novels what Marlow says of colonization in *Heart of Darkness*. "What redeems it is the idea only. An idea at the back of it . . . and an unselfish belief in the idea—something you can set up, and bow down before, and offer a sacrifice to" (p. 51). The idea and the manifold forces that oppose it lie at the heart of Conrad's dramas. Repeatedly invoked but never strictly specified, the faith is a version, combining both practical prowess and ideal meaning, of the Victorian spirit Conrad cherishes in his adopted land. This spirit, a seaman's translation of Matthew Arnold's "culture," incorporates the value, mandate, and shelter of that "firm conviction in the truth of ideas racially our own, in whose name are established the order, the morality of an ethical progress" (p. 339) that Marlow's correspondent in *Lord Jim* sets against Jim's romantic egotism. All Conrad's stories tell of threats and challenges that imperil belief, of flaws within and horrors without. But Conrad assumes that his readers will react to his equivocal tales and ironic strategies through the reflexes of their culture's truth: that, like the correspondent, they will take the high ground of the idea.

The essential thrust of each of the so-called political novels is to push the reader off from this safe ground. The effect of the multiple ironies and of the fundamental technique that Ian Watt terms "delayed decoding" is to subvert easy recourse to the idea.[1] Both the sardonic references to Marlow's stolid listeners and the fond but condescending irony surrounding the chief accountant, French lieutenant, and Captain Mitchell derive from Conrad's sense of the inertia and moral exiguousness that have overtaken the drama of an ethical progress. Conrad believes absolutely in the necessity of the idea. Without it, we are engulfed in horror. But this very belief depicts the hollowness of present culture as a nemesis to all that we have achieved and hold dear. The novels work to reconstitute the realities that necessitate moral civilization. Conrad strives to recompel the imagination of culture by forcing it to relive the disorder, ambiguity, and final loss of meaning that precede and hover round the enclave of our idea. To do this, he must subject his readers' firm convictions to the threatening challenges of truths beyond the pale. The novels I discuss become, in Cedric Watts's description, "Janiform," "two-faced," "centrally or importantly paradoxical or self-contradictory" because they imitate so immediately the immersion in cosmic irony, psychological ambiguity, and the villainous heroism of an overreaching dream that Marlow experiences in *Heart of Darkness*.[2]

Marlow is, of course, an exceptional figure, a hero in his own right. What Albert Guerard calls his "journey within" is one of the great tales of modern psychological adventure.[3] The extensive body of interpretation to which the short novel has given rise attests to the almost mythic force of Conrad's creation. But the one dimension of Marlow's story that has been little discussed is its sources in, and radical revision of, the kind of novel of education that Scott constructs in *Waverley*. The Congo bears many of the meanings that Scott assigns to the Highlands; Kurtz's role resembles that of Fergus M'Ivor, the Highland epic chieftain. Though Marlow is strong where Edward Waverley is passive, both men's experience is meant to serve as a model for the education demanded by their time. Scott's novel includes men who exemplify this education and whose presence helps guide Waverley from the glamorous yet disastrous romance of unmediated sublimity to the virtuous beauty of "real history" with its blending of prosaic actuality and moral culture. By contrast, Marlow's experience seems to teach permanent imbalance and uncertainty. His epoch offers neither a vital moral curriculum nor exemplars of the idea. Instead, there are hollow men who deprive culture of mandate and meaning. The idea has become incorporated in and enmeshed with horror. Truth and abomination are interwoven in Kurtz, who expresses "some sort of belief" in "the appalling face of a glimpsed truth" (p. 151). The education that must prepare Marlow to become himself a teacher—the ambiguous sage of ambiguity we encounter on the *Nellie*—must confront the insidious example of culture's faithless pilgrims and the grand enigma of Kurtz. Waverley acquires the tempering and fulfilling truths of an order, a *Bildung*, that combines the prosaic and poetic; Marlow's lesson leads only to his celebrated comment that "it was something to have at least a choice of nightmares" (p. 138).

Yet clearly the understanding underlying this remark is a product of the education acquired by Waverley and by many later protagonists of Victorian moral realism. From the beginning of his narrative, Marlow's comments and judgments rest upon the birthright of Victorian moral culture. The story Marlow tells involves the necessary education of this birthright by the lessons of nightmare. The crux of the training will be, not the equivocal association with Kurtz, but the outrageously demanding examination conducted by Kurtz's Intended. When Marlow visits her, he is still a fascinated captive of nightmare. "The vision seemed to enter the house with me . . . the heart of a conquering darkness. It was a moment of triumph for the wilderness, an invading and vengeful rush which, it seemed to me, I would have to keep back alone for the salvation of another soul" (pp. 155–56). But the Intended is not just another soul, though in the soulless world of Marlow's recent experience this would be a rare distinction. Like such later women as Emilia Gould, Antonia Avellanos, and Nathalie Haldin, she is both an embodiment of the social and moral romantic idealism of the idea—a sentimental transformation of Conrad's father's utopianism—and the vulnerable, dependent bride of the idea's practical strength. "She had a mature capacity for fidelity, for belief, for suffering. The room seemed to have grown darker, as if all the sad light of the cloudy evening had taken refuge on her forehead. This fair hair, this pale visage, this pure brow, seemed surrounded by an ashy halo from which the dark eyes looked out at me. Their glance was guileless, profound, confident, and trustful" (p. 157). The picture recalls the frame narrator's initial vision of the gloom gathered round London, the source of civilizing light, "the greatest town on earth" (p. 45). As her generalized title implies, the Intended is less a person than a human role: she is the faith that must be protected and cherished; she is the ideal that truth must wed in order to become moral civilization. Dispossessed by Kurtz, she calls on Marlow, who must plight his troth to a kind of *fino amore*. However "halting and wooden" the ensuing dialogue,[4] it becomes the rankling test of what Marlow can make of an education from which he can no longer derive clear lessons.

The encounter demands a true, knightly laureate; Marlow can only be a self-conscious Quixote. From any traditional point of view he fails his test. He who so pointedly abominates lies must shelter the Intended's faith by telling her that Kurtz died with her name—rather than the appallingly ambiguous invocation: "The horror! The horror!"—on his lips. Marlow bows "before the faith that was in her, before that great and saving illusion that shone with an unearthly glow in the darkness, in the triumphant darkness from which I could not have defended her—from which I could not even defend myself" (p. 159). Abashed by an impossible necessity, Marlow enters the characteristic dilemma of Conrad's major novels. The atmosphere of his predicament is an unstable chiaroscuro, a conjunction of dark fact and moral faith. No action is possible. There are only words—those words that the narrator of *Under Western Eyes* will label "the great foes of reality" (p. 3). Marlow is now, like Kurtz, a voice. The Intended pleads: Kurtz's "words, at least, have not died." Marlow grimly agrees: both the man and his words "will remain."

(pp. 160–61)
> "She put out her arms as if after a retreating figure, stretching them black and with clasped pale hands across the fading and narrow sheen of the window. Never see him! I saw him clearly enough then. I shall see this eloquent phantom as long as I live, and I shall see her, too, a tragic and familiar Shade, resembling in this gesture another one, tragic also, and bedecked with powerless charms, stretching bare brown arms over the glitter of the infernal stream, the stream of darkness. She said suddenly very low, 'He died as he lived.'
>
> " 'His end,' said I, with dull anger stirring in me, 'was in every way worthy of his life.' "

Marlow's equivocations and lies—we remember that he has also lied on Kurtz's behalf—parallel the refusal of straight-forwardness in his narrative technique. Both convey the destructive element in which moral meaning must now be immersed: the corroded and corroding syllabus of an ironic education. The Intended blurs into Kurtz's native consort; Marlow overlaps Kurtz; the darkness flows into—is, indeed, necessary to—the light. The configurations, doublings, inversions, and echoes; the cross-currents and cross-purposes; the dislocations of time, place, and language: all these express the factual and moral uncertainty that besets any act of narrative understanding, let alone of instruction. Yet Conrad remains as much a Victorian as a modern. The idea remains. But it undergoes a highly questionable alchemy into "that great and saving illusion" that still glows in a darkling world. The idea loses the tangible structures and supports that once defined it and becomes sheerly a faith resting on the evidence of things not seen, the substance of things hoped for. As the truth of God is contained in the paradoxes of faith, so the truth of the idea becomes a mystery. But Conrad distrusts mystery and keeps his distance from the habits of mind fundamental to religion. For him the fact of truth as fiction, of the idea as illusion, sets the stage for irony upon irony. Ethical progress is a true dream. But since it is a dream, a lie, an ideal fiction, how are we to dissociate its mandate from that inspiring Jim's dream, Charles Gould's dream, or the dreams of revolutionism? Not only are these false dreams the secret sharers of moral illusionism; they are in their faith just as true.

Irony and conviction are so interwoven in Conrad's best novels that it becomes impossible to say which elicits or doubles which. The ironic temper of Conrad's work eludes such valuable definitions of the varieties and strategies of irony as those provided by D. C. Muecke and Wayne C. Booth.[5] The irony shapes all aspects of the personality of the novels I discuss. The mode of theme, action, and technique that results is suggested by Jonathan Culler's general remarks about Flaubert's ironic drama of uncertainty.

> *Irony both undercuts and promotes the activity of interpretation. On the one hand, its most frequent targets are views of a situation*

> which it suggests are foolish, deficient, or otherwise at odds with the "facts." . . . If irony as a mode carries any single warning it is that concluding is dangerous. But on the other hand . . . many of the delights come from the call to interpretation that it issues. An ironic sentence, by definition, requires the interpreter to prove his own ingenuity in supplying an absent meaning; and it is thus a form of language which defers and tantalizes, which confers importance on the process of interpretation, while simultaneously bearing implicit warning of its dangers.[6]

Most of these comments can be applied to Conrad's procedures. But the suggestions of an aesthetic or linguistic game, however serious, would be out of place. Conrad's large share in the pessimism of much turn-of-the-century thought leads him to conceive human action as taking place against the background of cosmic or general irony: as flies to wanton boys, so are our needs and aspirations to the powers that create both us and our situation. The interpretations elicited by Conrad's irony are our only hope of holding back our fate. However playful, antic, or fantastic, the irony undertakes a dubious battle on an uncertain ground for the salvation of our souls.

Such a statement, of course, recalls Conrad's voice at its highest pitch. The work of irony and interpretation is desperate, but it usually compounds the poetic with the prosaic, idealism with cliché. The absolutistic resonance of the drama that Marlow, Kurtz, and the Intended act out sounds in the subsequent novels amid the noise of the commonplace. The situation Conrad depicts is much like that of Chief Inspector Heat in *The Secret Agent* when he discovers both that his "safe" anarchists have committed a murderous outrage and that his own superior mistrusts his ability to unravel the mystery.

(pp. 116–17)
> He had discovered in this affair a delicate and perplexing side, forcing upon the discoverer a certain amount of insincerity—that sort of insincerity which, under the names of skill, prudence, discretion, turns up at one point or another in most human affairs. He felt at the moment like a tight-rope artist might feel if suddenly, in the middle of the performance, the manager of the Music Hall

> *were to rush out of the proper managerial seclusion and begin to shake the rope. Indignation, the sense of moral insecurity engendered by such a treacherous proceeding joined to the immediate apprehension of a broken neck, would, in the colloquial phrase, put him in a state. And there would be also some scandalized concern for his art, too, since a man must identify himself with something more tangible than his own personality, and establish his pride somewhere, either in his social position, or in the quality of the work he is obliged to do, or simply in the superiority of the idleness he may be fortunate enough to enjoy.*

General irony mocks the relation between valuable human dedication and the circumstances that govern it. Verbal and situational ironies abound. The Chief Inspector's pride in his work, which one might expect to be treated with the serious respect Conrad accords his many faithful seamen, is deflated at the end by association with the idle rich and with the theme of demonic inertia elsewhere embodied in Mr. Verloc. Overarching these ironies is the ironic perspective itself, a sardonic superiority resembling (in yet another irony) that of the manager, which presents anarchists, terrorists, double agents, police, and even decent citizens such as Winnie, her mother, and brother as something close to the puppets that Thackeray's stage manager returns to their box at the end of *Vanity Fair*. The characters are all tiny fictions living ridiculous illusions. Yet not only does the Chief Inspector's situation epitomize Conrad's view of the human condition; the Chief Inspector's art mirrors Conrad's own. The craft of protection and the art that would emulate it are simultaneously essential and absurd.

The self-consciousness that acknowledges faith and its folly, that presents illusion and actuality on the same narrative plane, is best suggested through the elusive concept termed *romantic irony*. The complexity of recent efforts to map this ambiguous terrain makes summary difficult, but Conrad's art surely parallels the spirit underlying D. C. Muecke's general description. Romantic irony is

> *the irony of the fully-conscious artist whose art is the ironical presentation of the ironic position of the fully-conscious artist. The artist is in an ironic position for several reasons: in order to write*

> well he must be both creative and critical, subjective and objective, enthusiastic and realistic, emotional and rational, unconsciously inspired and a conscious artist; his work purports to be about the world and yet is a fiction; he feels an obligation to give a true or complete account of reality but he knows this is impossible, reality being incomprehensibly vast, full of contradictions, and in a continual state of becoming, so that even a true account would be immediately falsified as soon as it was completed. The only possibility open for a real artist is to stand apart from his work and at the same time incorporate this awareness of his ironic position into the work itself and so create something which will, if a novel, not simply be a story but rather the telling of a story complete with the author and the narrating, the reader and the reading, the style and the choosing of the style, the fiction and its distance from fact, so that we shall regard it as being ambivalently both art and life.[7]

Clearly, this irony is well qualified to express our contemporary distrust of literature and language: to dramatize the reflexes of what Nathalie Sarraute calls "the age of suspicion." But though Conrad's irony is close enough to our distrust to have invited close scrutiny under its key signature, his fully conscious service is to the idea of moral culture. Since the idea can no longer be represented as fact, it becomes a creation of the ethical imagination: an art.

Conrad's special version of romantic irony is elicited by the ambiguities hemming in the art of culture: ambiguities treated by Hardy, Gide, Mann, Lawrence, and many other late nineteenth-century and early modern writers. The idea of such culture carries with it perilous perplexities about human values, rights, and purposes. Yet against all opposing evidence it must perform an act of faith similar to that Emilia Gould would practice upon material interests and the silver that supports them in *Nostromo*. By "her imaginative estimate of its power she endowed that lump of metal with a justificative conception, as though it were not a mere fact, but something far-reaching and impalpable, like the true expression of an emotion or the emergence of a principle" (p. 107). Such a version of the service undertaken by Conrad's art, however, is too abstract and, in the words Marlow applies to his aunt's idealism, "too beautiful altogether." Much as many American romances both accept the emotions cherished by sensibility and strive to dissociate their action from its feminized principles by locating it in a world of men without women, Conrad's irony—in one of its least engaging qualities—portrays women's moral romanticism as powerless to cope with the demands that realities place upon faith. "It's queer," Marlow continues, "how out of touch with truth women are. They live in a world of their own. . . . and if they were to set it up it would go to pieces before the first sunset. Some confounded fact we men have been living contentedly with ever since the day of creation would start up and knock the whole thing over" (p. 59). From the Intended to Nathalie Haldin, Conrad's respect for women's truth will result in ever stronger and ever sadder stories. But women's faith remains a grail to be blessed with and protected, not a model for the bravery that art must undertake. On the other hand, those men—a French lieutenant or a Captain Mitchell—who serve truth while living contentedly with fact offer no better hope; their dedication is grounded in what Marlow refers to in *Lord Jim* as "the saving dullness" (p. 276). The burden placed upon Conrad's self-conscious, self-challenging romantic irony is to integrate Mrs. Gould's justificative conception, the blind dedication of loyal service, and the constant and ambiguous, tempting and anarchic forces that contest moral achievement.

At any given moment one of these components holds sway over the others. Each novel is an ironic kaleidoscope whose intention is to be derived from the sum of multiple single views. Full awareness is displaced by the interpretations demanded by an immediate situation. But of course the narrative voice must know the whole picture. And immediacy must be achieved by dissembling this knowledge. Conrad's narrative personas and Marlow in particular are forced repeatedly to adapt the ironic strategies of the *eirōn*, the dissembler: a necessity that helps explain the crucial function of doublings and echoing half views. Situations that exact the full self-consciousness of dissimulation become the exemplary moments of romantic irony. Confronted in *Lord Jim* by Jewel's utter dread, by her unquenchable fear that Jim will desert her and compel her "to die weeping," Marlow is stricken both by his knowledge of

Jim's past untrustworthiness and by his vision of an "irremediable horror" in the nature of life. "For a moment I had a view of a world that seemed to wear a vast and dismal aspect of disorder, while, in truth, thanks to our unwearied efforts, it is as sunny an arrangement of small conveniences as the mind of man can conceive.... I seemed to have lost all my words in the chaos of dark thoughts I had contemplated for a second or two beyond the pale. These came back, too, very soon, for words also belong to the sheltering conception of light and order which is our refuge" (p. 313). Assuring Jewel that nothing can tear Jim from her side, Marlow denies fact to preserve faith. Lying for Kurtz, he insists upon the facts that make faith necessary. Juggling fact and faith, the truth of darkness and the true fiction of light, each of the novels combines subversion with subterfuge. And the cost of Conrad's narrative service to illusion is painfully increased by this double agency of irony.

Indeed, Razumov's double life in *Under Western Eyes* may be read as a tragic account of a world, life, and art betrayed by unavoidable ironies. Marlow's comment about words anticipates what comes increasingly to seem the real horror. Words affirm the fictionality that is our refuge, but particularly in *The Secret Agent* and *Under Western Eyes* words start to appear as the faithless, hollow, or perverted pilgrims of moral art. Instead of "bringing to light the truth, manifold and one,"[8] language becomes an instrument of cosmic irony. Words seem to lead an existence of their own, toying with and mocking the narrative goal Marlow proclaims on board the *Nellie*: "to convey the life-sensation" of experience, "that which makes its truth, its meaning" (p. 82). In response to the insidious irony of language, the narrative voice of *The Secret Agent* accepts the challenge of an outrageous verbal tightrope act. Conscious meaninglessness and inversion are set against the horror of an endemic linguistic deviltry, much as the detectives would subvert the law in order to uphold it. By the end of *Under Western Eyes*, Conrad's irony becomes so convoluted, beset, and suspicious of itself that it is forced to seek the shelter of truths beyond the pale of irony—of truths in which it cannot have faith.

What makes an account of the principles and sentiments of Conrad's irony so difficult is the competition between the romantic irony of cultural faith and a quite different ironic perspective. The self-conscious illusionism of the former explains much, but an explanation along its lines is often balked by the satiric, even cruel irony that mocks the present condition of culture. The reflexes of distaste can make the "conception of light and order which is our refuge" seem a bitter burlesque. The kind of outrage so common in contemporary exposés of failed values and their hypocritical pawns smolders alongside Conrad's light. To lie, as Marlow says, is abominable; he accepts the abomination for the sake of a true faith. Yet if, as Conrad's sardonic glimpses of the way things are so frequently imply, this faith serves only a questionable confidence game, then the burdens of romantic irony become themselves subject to a black or absurdist irony.

Conrad's satiric animus never quite overcomes his idea, but it casts his stories into a potentially dangerous state of interpretative tension. *Heart of Darkness* pits the fierce reality of Kurtz's egotism against the compelling truth of the Intended's fidelity. But the exemplary force of both the nightmare and the dream, and of Marlow's role as pupil of each, must somehow soar free of the satiric spectacle to which Conrad devotes so much attention. Kurtz's grandeur arises out of the faithless petty demonism that Marlow so ruthlessly mocks. The Intended's ideal devotion apotheosizes the half-admirable, half-ridiculous service of the chief accountant and the callow adoration of the Russian seaman who idolizes Kurtz. Faith and folly—as Winnie Verloc and her brother will so distressingly prove—are tangled in a single knot.

The ironies that protect and teach mingle with those that scorn to create the mixture of weighty narration and dismissive disdain in Marlow's approach to his sedentary listeners aboard the *Nellie*. A similar compounding marks not just Marlow's storytelling in *Lord Jim* but also the narrative voices in Conrad's later novels. If the larger-than-life actors in *Heart of Darkness* cannot escape the conflation of contradictory ironies, the far less exalted protagonists Conrad goes on to treat will be even more vulnerable. Not just in the modes of expression they come to adopt, but at their very source, romantic and satiric irony invade each other. Jim is a foolish, childish dreamer not unlike Kurtz's Russian admirer; he is a figure of transcendent faith not unlike the Intended. Jim's fiction leads to moral treason; his fidelity to the fiction shines as a bright light in a shady world. These opposing interpretations, moreover, involve Conrad's own divided allegiances: his attitude toward Jim's dream of glory and adventure, toward dreams and imagination in general, and toward those who cannot dream or who defame dreams. Attraction, self-rebuke for the attraction, and scorn for those who are not attracted exist simultaneously. They lead to the complex tone of Marlow's reference to our "sunny conveniences" and to the conjoined mockery and relief in his comment, just after Jewel forces him to glance beyond the pale: "I went back into my shell directly" (p. 313). Marlow's sardonic awareness that the refuge of our idea is an illusion is appropriate to one kind of irony; his attitude toward those who need, acquiesce in, or complacently inhabit this refuge stems from a different ironic source. The two come together when he remarks that Jewel "should have made for herself a shelter of inexpugnable peace out of [Jim's] honest affection. She had not the knowledge—not the skill perhaps" (p. 313). Jewel, the *Patna* pilgrims, the tourists at the hotel where Marlow and Jim converse, and numerous others in the novel are incapable of the skillful interplay romantic irony demands. To satirize such simplicity and dependency as hollowness may reinforce the appeal of Jim's private dream of full devotion, but it also confuses the moral truth ascribed to the code. Marlow, of course, is not Conrad. The character's belittling satire is not the author's. Yet the mockery and disdain frequently directed at those who cannot live without the support of illusion suggest what is perhaps the greatest challenge that Conrad's art of ironic protection will face in the next three novels.

The challenge lies at the heart of the essential action dramatized in *Nostromo*. This "most anxiously meditated of the longer novels" (p. vii) chronicles the attempted alchemy of material interests into a version of the idea, Emilia Gould's "ideal conception," and the brave effort to turn the idea into a functional Realpolitik. Satiric smallness must be raised to the illusionary greatness of moral civilization. Opportunities for competing ironies are pervasive. The very title, by casting the Capataz de Cargadores as the register of the alchemy Mrs. Gould envisages, places the superficiality and vanity of a common seaman at the center of the novel's stage.

Nostromo's simplicity makes him an ideal reader of illusion. He is the factotum of the idea. His perfect service to "something more tangible than his own personality" grants him a wholly fulfilling public identity. Acting with panache on behalf of the practical necessities of the newborn republic, he is no longer hollow, no longer a satiric model of foolish vanity. But Nostromo's moral neutrality, like the crude fact of the silver, contains the irreducible dross of mereness. When the fiction that the Goulds and their allies would erect upon his service deconstructs, the Capataz is cast back from illusion into a kind of satiric pathos of nonentity. He was the coin validated by the treasury of a dream; he dies a counterfeit. Mrs. Gould, Dr. Monygham, and Linda Viola, in their fidelity and its betrayal, convey Conrad's continuing empathy with the pain of those who depend upon a moral faith at odds with fact. But Nostromo's reversion to unadorned materialism and egotism anticipates the bitter devolution of the terms of Conrad's irony that takes place in *The Secret Agent*: romantic irony must mine its sheltering truth out of coarse, often repellent ore.

In the Verlocs' London the glamour of challenging service festers in landlocked banality. The idea and the equivocal nature of its refuge remain all-important. But in the ironic muddle of duplicity, counterfeiting, and grotesquerie that *The Secret Agent* portrays, the grand thematic chiaroscuro that surrounds the Congo, Patusan, and Costaguana becomes a foul murk. Up close, the heartland of culture emanates a moral unsavoriness not unlike the stench of rotted hippo: a smell that almost overpowers the irony of culture as saving art. The uncharming Winnie and her simple-minded brother carry the pathos of human insufficiency to the verge of absurdity. The idea of sheltering statecraft is mocked by the caricatural Home Minister and by the mixed motives of the police. The enemies of the idea are not private dreamers like Jim, nor horrors like Kurtz or Gentleman Brown, nor tyrants like those who figure in Don José Avellanos's *Fifty Years of Misrule*; the nemesis to moral illusion is now the sleazy hollowness of a specious anarchy and the entropic inertia of a Mr. Verloc. A disfigured world mocks the idea; Conrad's irony can only succeed by mocking the mockery. Protection, shelter, and value are everywhere debased.

Through hyperbole, satiric inversion, and the devices of grotesque melodrama, irony must insinuate the opposing secret agency of the idea; it must perform the function that the officials bungle and Mr. Verloc defames. But in accepting this task, the high service of irony is pressed to its limits. Self-conscious illusionism finds itself untenably close to the distasteful fictions of mock-anarchy. The strength of culture is no longer a fine truth, but something resembling the antlike toil of the London masses so feared by the terrorist Professor.

The irony of *The Secret Agent* displaces horror into a dark burlesque and the idea into an ungainly avatar of Mrs. Gould's grand conception. The miserable fate of Stevie and Winnie gives pain, not instruction, because the two are such denuded vehicles of ethical truth. Fact and faith both lend themselves to demeaning illustration. And behind the minimal refuge irony can suggest lies despair: the death of illusion's words and meaning. Conrad's quixotic compound is as perilously at hazard as the tightrope artist. There may be no viable idea, no net. The windmill that ironic art transforms into a sheltering giant may be only a crude windmill after all.

This undercurrent of nihilistic absurdity is institutionalized into the Russian autocracy and impotent revolutionism that suck the life out of human meaning in *Under Western Eyes*. The rather Prufrockian English teacher who narrates the story of Razumov and the Haldins tries his best to soften the unutterable desolation that Russia embodies: to translate it into a fact that Western truth can comprehend. But the teacher is no Marlow; his beliefs, satiric thrusts, and ironies cannot reconstitute the moral value—only the craven safety—of our shell. Neither the narrator nor the shopworn decencies of Genevan refuge can escape the satire emphasized by the supreme drama in their midst. The nation that governs this drama is a black hole swallowing all the hopes and devices of moral education. The absolute fact forbids even irony. As the "woman revolutionist" Sophia Antonovna tells Razumov: "women, children, and revolutionists hate irony, which is the negation of all saving instincts, of all faith, of all devotion, of all action" (p. 279).

The final irony is the bankruptcy of the irony that supports Conrad's finest achievements. Conrad conceives of his irony's task as masculine: an exercise of the strength that can face horror, endure ambiguity and self-doubts, and still keep faith with the high art that is the great and saving illusion of our culture. The horror epitomized by Russia reduces us all to the dependent weakness of women and children. We are all akin to Jewel, Nostromo, and Stevie. Revolt is impossible. All the strong men and revolutionists in *Under Western Eyes* enact tyranny or disaster. No doubt the destitution of heroic full consciousness that the novel conveys bears some relation to the breakdown Conrad underwent during the long years of composition.[9] But the terrible toll exacted by Conrad's difficult ironies is evident from *Heart of Darkness* onward. Russia does not, of course, destroy the faith upon which both Conrad's greatest and his lesser works rest. Rather, it emasculates the ironic temper of the great art, transforming ironic faith into sentimental endurance. In the impasse of Russia, women begin to take over from men as protagonists of the idea. And given Conrad's dismissive attitude toward women as practical forces, the reversal of role is accompanied by something like the dull, satiric anger Marlow feels when lying to the Intended—an anger that makes *Chance* so uncomfortable a novel. The descendants of the Intended are now cast in what was Marlow's role. Marlow's passing comment about Jewel comes to emerge as Conrad's truth: "Women find their inspiration in the stress of moments that for [men] are merely awful, absurd, or futile" (p. 315). Brave women are to be the golden bough and the wielders of the bough; their charm is to be the force that lights our way. Yet as we see in the concluding passages of *Under Western Eyes*, with their bitter mockery of Peter Ivanovitch and his hateful feminism, the new refuge elicits Conrad's satiric bent rather than the protection of his heroic irony.

I

LORD JIM
Irony and Dream

IN LEAPING FROM THE *Patna*, Jim betrays his nurture. He falls from the structured realm of public values and trust into the mystery of private reflexes and dreams. In so doing, he seems to set in motion what Guerard terms an "interior novel."[1] But for Marlow, and more extensively for Conrad, the story of this one psyche becomes a forum for the investigation of public faith. "The mystery of his attitude," Marlow insists, "got hold of me as though he had been an individual in the forefront of his kind, as if the obscure truth involved were momentous enough to affect mankind's conception of itself" (p. 93). Like Kurtz, Jim exists within the concern that preoccupies Conrad's major fiction: the authenticity and viability of the organic community to which Western civilization has sworn fidelity. Jim is a by-blow of this community: half in, half out. His father is a safe and staid clergyman; we know nothing of his mother, but may imagine her as an avatar of that veiled Eastern bride who rewards Jim's dream. Traditional value and romantic dream collide and then collude. By itself, each context is quite straightforward. But it is precisely the simplicity and direct appeal of both sides of Jim's dilemma, the near-featurelessness of his understanding of both, that make the terms of his embattled example contagious to others—as the series of doublings and identifications running from Brierly to Gentleman Brown demonstrates.[2] The values and shortcomings of Jim's upbringing and of his dream invest his example with the momentous possibility of meaning that Marlow intuits.

The first half of the novel investigates the truth of public value; the second half, the fantasy and melodrama of the misty romance of Patusan, flirts with dream. In both sections Marlow's puzzlement about Jim involves many of the questions that underlie Dowell's perplexity about sexual behavior in Ford Madox Ford's *The Good Soldier*. What one thought one knew and the stable existence one built upon the knowledge are illusions. Seeing Jim for the first time as he stands accused of deserting his trust, Marlow comments: "I liked his appearance; I knew his appearance; he came from the right place; he was one of us. He stood there for all the parentage of his kind, for men and women by no means clever or amusing, but whose very existence is based upon honest faith, and upon the instinct of courage" (p. 43). Jim's leap belies his appearance and the assumptions Marlow bases on his seeming decency. And on these assumptions, as we hear time and time again in *Lord Jim*, rests the faith that must order civilized endeavor. Dowell's disillusionment in Ford's novel is analogous. He has believed in a code of decency in sexual matters and implicitly connected this code with the very existence of moral civilization. When he discovers his wife's and his friend's adulteries, human behavior suddenly seems to him a maelstrom of ravening lusts. Faith topples into rending bafflement. "If for nine years I have possessed a goodly apple that is rotten at the core and discover its rottenness only in nine years . . . isn't it true to say that for nine years I possessed a goodly apple?"[3] Is all conventionally honest faith a mere facade? Is its cultural ethos merely specious? If so, is there any guide to existence? Does the "greatness" that the outcast Jim achieves in Patusan or the "goodness" of Dowell's adulterous friend contain a new knowledge or value that might offer some alternative to what has been lost?

As we shall see, the romance of Patusan and the counterpoint between Jim's monochord idealism and the cultural value Conrad comes to place in irony lead *Lord Jim* in directions far different from those Ford pursues. But the similar scope of Conrad's and Ford's novels provides a suggestive point of departure. Jim's indecent desertion and the sexual indecency of Ford's characters are comments on the values of their civilization. The ideal ethos of education, duty, and communal purpose in which earlier Victorian generations believed has become Dowell's goodly apple. The code of seamanship in Conrad and that of Tory manners in Ford embody what Marlow calls "the sheltering conception of light and order which is our refuge" (p. 313). Ford presents the violation of his code with extreme pessimism and in the rhetoric of final things. "Someone has said that the death of a mouse from cancer is the whole sack of Rome by the Goths, and I swear to you that the breaking up of our little four-square coterie was such another unthinkable event."[4] Though Conrad's perspective is more equivocal, the potential ramifications of Jim's leap are no less extreme. Marlow seeks "some convincing shadow of an excuse" for Jim's act because he hopes to lay "what is the most obstinate ghost of man's creation, . . . the uneasy doubt uprising like a mist, secret and gnawing like a worm, and more chilling than the certitude of death—the doubt of the sovereign power enthroned in a fixed standard of conduct" (p. 50).

Jim is "no mean traitor"; his betrayal of his trust is "a breach of faith with the community of mankind" (p. 157). Like adultery in Ford, infidelity in Conrad is a crime against moral civilization. But in both novels the crimes insinuate an insufficiency in traditional standards that opens the way for personal desires and dreams. In *Lord Jim*, Jim's treason is in part made comprehensible, even ambiguously made sympathetic, by the hollowness of inherited values. Marlow's initial evocation of the honest faith Jim ought to serve is markedly defensive. Our ethical nurture fosters "an unthinking and blessed stiffness before the outward and inward terrors, before the might of nature, and the seductive corruption of men—[a stiffness] backed by a faith invulnerable to the strength of facts, to the contagion of example, to the solicitation of ideas" (p. 43). Marlow's comments on this faith range from his sardonic mockery of the tourists at the hotel where he talks with Jim to respect for the stiff courage of the French lieutenant and Bob Stanton. But both fools and heroes live lives sequestered from the whole truth of the human situation. The uncomfortable irony that characterizes Marlow's tone strains to mediate between faith and fact, between the illusion that protects and the need to confront things as they are. Jim's private stiffness is as devoid of irony as that of civilization's truest believers. But the personal has an immediacy and an appeal that public belief has long since lost. And Jim's story, wending its way between the simple fascination of an individual's romantic dream and the self-protective blindness of public illusion, engages Marlow because it appears to be a straightforward, real-life instance of the irony inherent in the human condition.

Marlow's irony is an attempt on Conrad's part to elude the force of pessimism. As Peter J. Glassman observes, in "*Lord Jim* . . . the universe itself seems organized in barely surreptitious, virtually animate opposition to human expectations and needs."[5] As a fact, Jim's leap confirms the pessimistic appraisal of nature that Royal Roussel equates with the idea of darkness in Conrad.[6] But just as Jim's dream of ultimate triumph refuses pessimism, so Marlow's irony complicates and tempers the loose Schopenhauerian view that would interpret the action as an instance of human delusion adrift in cosmic indifference. A defensive irony works as a kind of fifth column within the bleak atmosphere of cosmic irony. Jim is a straggler from moral order, but the flaws in this order allow Marlow to entertain the possibility that Jim may be a harbinger of better things to come. Though Jim is simple to the point of flatness, the fate he dreams for himself is in its way parallel to the early modern vision of self-creation: to the idea of selfhood as art in Proust or the great Gatsby's desire to live out a platonic idea of himself. However ingenuous Jim's romantic heroism and his dedication to its adventure, his goals are truer—more "sincere" in Gide's sense of the word—than the goals to which most of the other characters attend.

This hopeful possibility is of course set starkly against the disorder Jim spawns. The dream is quite as much a threat as an example. By desiring to go it alone, Jim undercuts the bonds of moral community. These bonds may be illusions, but the illusion they represent may finally be the necessary paradox inherent in the maintenance of moral meaning in a dark world. The pain of things makes illusion real. Commenting on Jewel's appalling distrust of Jim in Patusan, on her plea not to "die weeping," Marlow acknowledges that "the passive, irremediable horror of the scene"

(p. 313) "*had the power to drive me out of my conception of existence, out of that shelter each of us makes for himself to creep under in moments of danger, as a tortoise withdraws within its shell. For a moment I had a view of a world that seemed to wear a vast and dismal aspect of disorder. . . . But still—it was only a moment: I went back into*

> *my shell directly. One must—don't you know?—though I seemed to have lost all my words in the chaos of dark thoughts I had contemplated for a second or two beyond the pale. These came back, too, very soon, for words also belong to the sheltering conception of light and order which is our refuge."*

Beyond the sheltering pale is a literally unspeakable disorder—which is why Kurtz's naming of the horror is presented as a kind of victory. Jim flies in the face of the grimly sardonic conception of the necessity of culture as refuge that is implicit in Marlow's "*must.*" Marlow's strained belief in shelter is ambiguous enough to permit the off-chance of Jim's success. But the odds against such success are as vast and dismal as the fact of primal chaos.

Marlow's account of Jim is by no means the whole of Conrad's story. As Daniel R. Schwartz notes, Marlow moves toward Jim's position; "Marlow's epistemological quest culminates with the blurring of the distinction between objective and subjective experience."[7] Marlow is himself a character; behind his mediating irony we sense dimensions to Jim's example beyond his ken. The issues that frame *Lord Jim* involve far more than the distinction between objective and subjective: more even than the tension between Marlow's public conception of existence and Jim's private dream of heroic order. In taking Jim and Marlow as the focal points of a novel more ambitious than the dreamer could dream and more ironic than the narrator-ironist could achieve, Conrad is attempting to dramatize one of the most difficult aspects of the situation brought about by the erosion of traditional faiths. Primitive man, as E. R. Dodds reminds us in *The Greeks and the Irrational*, sought one kind of shelter in his religion and another kind in his conception of morality.[8] Religion comprehended and tried to placate the cruel force of final things; it made possible the existence of a humanity limited in knowledge and power within a mysterious field of forces alien to man. Morality, on the other hand, grew out of the needs of man's relations to man. Religion dealt with the absolute circumstances of man's position in the universe; morality, with the relative needs of communal purposes and stabilities. A hallmark of what we regard as a mature civilization is the blending of these two functions into the single fabric of moral religion. Conrad's consistent idealization of the code of seamanship, which is maintained, as Nadjer demonstrates, against much contradictory personal experience, and the impulse behind the less convincing exemplary role he invests in figures such as Singleton stem from an impulse to believe that the traditional world of "us"—the world of unwearied efforts—had achieved a working synthesis between social ethics and cosmic circumstances. Jim's leap carries him out of this synthesis; he lands in the position of those moderns who must become mythmakers because morality no longer responds adequately or authentically to the basic questions posed by our position in the universe. Conrad is deeply doubtful about both the validity and the viability of the modern dream of which Jim's dream is the lowest common denominator. Yet he allows Marlow a greater freedom of ambivalence than his own letters and essays usually permit. Marlow's inconclusive and ironic temper leaves a certain ambiguous opening for the blurring of distinctions. But however complex, Marlow's ironies are finally contained tensely within an omniscient irony about irony itself.

This larger scope is suggested in the strategy Conrad uses to begin the novel. In J. Hillis Miller's words, the "first part of the novel is told by an 'omniscient' narrator who seems like the narrator of a novel by Trollope or by George Eliot."[9] The first four chapters introduce Jim as the kind of romantic dreamer—a descendant of Scott's Waverley—that so many Victorian novels of moral realism and education instruct in the facts of what Scott terms "real history." Jim's "thoughts would be full of valorous deeds: he loved these dreams and the success of his imaginary achievements. They were the best parts of life, its secret truth, its hidden reality" (p. 20). The implied standard treats dreams and imagination as offshoots of untested youth. Jim has the potential for all the public school virtues; he simply requires the tempering experience that yields moral character. "He was gentlemanly, steady, tractable, with a thorough knowledge of his duties; and in time, when yet very young, he became chief mate of a fine ship, without ever having been tested by those events of the sea that show in the light of day the inner worth of a man . . . that reveal the quality of his resistance and the secret truth of his pretences, not only to others but also to himself" (p. 10). Both the content and the secure, summarizing tone are familiar. Jim's imaginings are in no sense original, let alone modern; his hoped-for heroism is that enshrined in "light holiday literature" (p. 5). It is no surprise that after being forced to leave his ship because of a slow-healing minor injury, he rejects the home service "with its harder conditions, severer view of duty, and the hazard of stormy oceans" (p. 13). "The charm of vagueness" (p. 20) that pervades his secret reality leads him to an easy berth on the *Patna*. Confronted with the apparently disastrous bulging bulkhead after the mysterious collision, his imagination takes flight and he leaps after it.

The opening chapters prepare us for the kind of yarn Marlow intuits when he first sees Jim at the court of inquiry. Behind the flawed man and the cursory facts may lie what Balzac terms a "secret history": the conjunction of private and public truths that so engages the traditional novelistic mentality. Jim's story promises a compelling variation upon a time-honored structure. But the underlying and exfoliating irony of Marlow's narrative involvement in Jim's situation derives from the fact that the traditional structure implied by Conrad's omniscient opening is as misleading as Jim himself. Moral realism proposes a synthesis of individual nature, objective circumstances, and communal or ethical truth. Narrative is based upon a fluctuating but finally morally instructive relation between the subjective and the objective. Almost from the very beginning Marlow is forced to question and to attempt to reenvisage this relation. As he so often repeats, he is fascinated by the "infernal alloy" (p. 45) in Jim's seemingly trustworthy cultural metal. His initial interest is in the alloy, in Jim's individual makeup, but this investigation leads insistently into doubts about the metal itself. And these doubts reflect back onto the question of Jim's nature.

The ironic perspective in which Marlow finds himself will cast the achievement of all meaning, individual and cultural, into perplexity. The terms of moral meaning in themselves are never in doubt. What Jim has betrayed is quite clear; he has failed the code of the home service: "its saving power, the grace of its secular right to our fidelity, to our obedience" (p. 222). What is now obscure is how the individual can internalize and honestly enact the moral values in which all the decent characters believe. The central position of this ironic obscurity accounts, I believe, for the introduction of Captain Brierly so near the beginning of Marlow's narrative. Brierly, one of the judges at the inquiry, is an impeccably successful young sailor whose "self-satisfaction presented . . . a surface as hard as granite. He committed suicide very soon after" (p. 58). Like the narrative omniscience with which the novel commences, Brierly seems a firm and convincing spokesman for traditional truth. The jarring conclusion of Marlow's brief comment has the same effect on Brierly's safeness as a spokesman as Jim's story will have on our ability to accept traditional power, grace, and right. No doubt, as Schwartz argues, Brierly's sudden intuition of kinship with Jim can be understood as a subjective explanation of his offer to pay Jim to disappear, and a further empathic identification with Jim's untested faith and its result helps explain the suicide.[10] But the effect of Brierly's presence at this point in the narrative is both to generalize Jim's flaw and to show how far out of joint any conventional appraisal of appearance and reality, ethos and personality, morality and dream, may be. Jim's desertion casts him outside the pale: a man without a country. But the bewildering situation of exile now includes the bewildering possibility that there may be no viable countries and no objective standard of patriotism.

Brierly's example, of course, is part of Marlow's rhetorical strategy. His seamen listeners are, we gather, unimaginative types. Quite apart from Marlow's slowly and complexly developing bond with Jim—the ambiguous identification discussed by Guerard, Schwartz, and others—his narrative can only convey the force of his sense of Jim's story by subverting his audience's fixed standards of understanding. The fact of Brierly's untrustworthiness is one tactic. Another is Marlow's shifting of the emphasis away from the public desertion to Jim's painful private situation. Having lost name, character, and the social defenses that accompany successful existence among others, Jim is naked. His pitiful state leads to his taking a reference to an offensive native pariah dog as a cur to be a personal insult. He has lost the saving power of the shell we can retreat into for safety. The pathetic view of Jim continues throughout the first half of the novel; we find it in the brief glimpses of Jim as a kind of Wandering Jew constantly in motion around Eastern ports. Yet since Marlow's concern is more with the obscurities of the truth of Jim's situation than with Jim himself, pity is employed as a permitting premise rather than as a main theme. Moreover, pity on the one hand and the subversive pessimism implicit in Brierly's suicide court a far too unambiguous reaction: the notion that we are all exiles, that the code we profess is hollow. To counter this simplistic negativism Marlow insists upon the appalling immorality of the company into which Jim has fallen—a point that will recur in full horror during the encounter with Gentleman Brown. Jim's act creates a nasty kinship with such true curs as the *Patna's* captain and other officers, the guano-mad Chester, and the senile quondam cannibal Robinson.

Against such outcasts and against the pathos of Jim's case Marlow holds up the words and example of the French lieutenant, an exemplary vicar of culture's "secular grace." He "reminded you of one of those snuffy, quiet village priests, into whose ears are poured the sins, the sufferings, the remorse of peasant generations, on whose faces the placid and simple expression is like a veil thrown over the mystery of pain and distress" (p. 139). Unlike the later references to the sunny conveniences of our sheltering code, Marlow's attitude toward the veil that the lieutenant helps hold in place seems unironic. There is even a hint that the lieutenant's blend of priestly wisdom and practical fidelity—the faith that accompanies him during his thirty hours on the unsafe *Patna*—mocks the growing entanglements of Marlow's interest in Jim. The lieutenant understands Jim's fear: we all feel it, he says. But desertion, turning tail, is another matter. "But the honour—the honour, monsieur! . . . The honour . . . that is real—that is!"; "when the honour is gone—*ah ça! par example*—I can offer no opinion—because—monsieur—I know nothing of it" (p. 148; Conrad's ellipses).

The lieutenant is the safest of all those who speak for the code of trust and decency. Yet his "stolid glibness" (p. 139) is another instance of the way in which "saving faith" has declined into "saving dullness" (p. 276). The Frenchman's idea of honor strips moral enterprise of glory; it is in its way as purblind as Jim's dream. And just before this episode Marlow complains of Jim's unawareness of the stakes his behavior involves. "I was aggrieved against him, as though he had cheated me—me!—of a splendid opportunity to keep up the illusion of my beginnings, as though he had robbed our common life of the last spark of its glamour" (p. 131). The lieutenant and those like him do not see what Marlow sees. As the exclamatory "me" suggests, Marlow's own dream is involved—is indeed the crucial narrative action—in Jim's dream. Jim's mystery broadens into the mystery of pain and distress in man's fate. Jim's situation engages the vast challenge that attends the idea of moral order as a faith, or a necessary illusion, willed into being against the odds of the human condition. Jim comes to seem the test of Marlow's hope that the work of moral shelter can repossess the heroic glamour that surrounds the dull Roman civilizers of pagan Britain in *Heart of Darkness*. For Marlow, the romance of Jim in Patusan borrows its force from the possibility of Jim's splendid opportunity: a possibility that the snuffy lieutenant and Marlow's stolid listeners cannot entertain. Both the attitude toward such dullness and the promise Jim enacts are clear in one of Marlow's several prefaces to his account of Jim in Patusan.

(p.225) *"My last words about Jim shall be few. I affirm he had achieved greatness; but the thing would be dwarfed in the telling, or rather in the hearing. Frankly, it is not my words that I mistrust but your minds. I could be eloquent were I not afraid you fellows had starved your imaginations to feed your bodies. I do not mean to be offensive; it is respectable to have no illusions—and safe—and profitable—and dull. Yet you, too, in your time must have known the intensity of life, that light of glamour created in the shock of trifles, as amazing as the glow of sparks struck from a cold stone—and as short-lived, alas!"*

The last lines associate Jim with the spirit that animates "Youth"; the last word recalls the ironic retrospect that in the short novel views this spirit askance. But the dream Jim lives out is far richer in cultural and, through its relation to Marlow, psychological connotations than anything in "Youth." Marlow's ironic temper, with its self-conscious hesitation between imagination and saving dullness, between language as vital engagement and language as shelter, has itself become a subject of Conrad's treatment of the condition of Western moral order. In Marlow's dream, the intensity of meaningful action condensed into the idea of glamour offers an alternative not only to the staidness that robs civilization of force but also to his own part in such passive safety. Indeed, Marlow's account of Jim in Patusan suggests in its near-envy a story told by one of the many overcivilized, overironic early moderns—the diverse kin of J. Alfred Prufrock—who covet the unmediated splendor of "real life."

Marlow's hope, and the justification for his engagement in Jim's fate, is that the dreamer's youth may restore the stirring force and enchantment of the early days of self and culture. But simply to affirm Jim is to disallow the hard-won ironies, ambiguities, and wisdom that accompany our shelter. If Jim is true, then our compromises and hesitations are false. Moreover, as Conrad's ever-insinuated omniscient irony places in question, Jim's personal flatness may be the fatal hazard of all youthful dreams. Can youth itself and Jim's youth in particular be more trustworthy crusaders for the dream than they were defenders of the faith? When after his long evening's talk with Marlow, Jim retreats from port to port seeking to keep himself intact for the opportunity he dreams of, Marlow has strong doubts. But "what I could never make up my mind about was whether his line of conduct amounted to shirking his ghost or to facing him out" (p. 197). The force of Marlow's increasing disenchantment is equivalent to the meaning he has invested in Jim. Jim's wayward movement strikes him as "hopeless, and poor Brierly's saying recurred to me, 'Let him creep twenty feet underground and stay there'" (p. 202).

Faced with the possibility that his involvement with Jim may prove as disastrous as Brierly's empathy, Marlow goes to consult Stein. Stein will speak for all the issues that the French lieutenant ignores—indeed, Guerard views the two counselors, each with his fractured English, as "pendant."[11] The retired dreamer sees Jim as a problem in a kind of existential poetics. Unlike the Frenchman, he views Jim as a particular type of individual, not as a member of a community of faith and honor. For romantic dreamers such as Jim, "the question is not how to get cured, but how to live" (p. 212). As David Thorburn has shown,[12] Stein's answer encapsulates the general wisdom of traditional romantic idealism: "That was the way. To follow the dream, and again to follow the dream" (pp. 214–15). These words, of course, provide the standard under which Jim advances into Patusan. The direction Jim will take is that into which Stein wanders when, at the conclusion of his talk with Marlow, he moves to the far end of his vast room. "It had an odd effect—as if these few steps had carried him out of this concrete and perplexed world. . . . his voice, heard in that remoteness where he could be glimpsed mysteriously busy with immaterial cares, was no longer incisive, seemed to roll voluminous and grave—mellowed by distance" (p. 213). Stein speaks out of and for the suggestive distance so dear to romantic art: "it was a charming and deceptive light, throwing the impalpable poesy of its dimness over pitfalls—over graves" (p. 215). The portals of this kind of dream close against the material cares, palpable facts, and perplexing objective challenges of the visible universe Conrad proposes to illuminate in the celebrated preface to *The Nigger of the "Narcissus."* Jim enters a spectral realm as remote from his parentage as that which awaits so many rebellious offspring of material culture in the fiction of Gide, Mann, Joyce, and others.

(p.216) *"At that moment it was difficult to believe in Jim's existence—starting from a country parsonage, blurred by crowds of men as by clouds of dust, silenced by the clashing claims of life and death in a material world—but his imperishable reality came to me with a convincing, with an irresistible force! I saw it vividly, as though in our progress through [Stein's] lofty silent rooms among fleeting gleams of light and the sudden revelations of human figures stealing with flickering flames within unfathomable and pellucid depths, we had approached nearer to absolute Truth, which, like Beauty itself, floats elusive, obscure, half submerged, in the silent still waters of mystery."*

. . .

In Patusan, Jim will approach Truth. He will seek to realize the Beauty of his dream. His Patusan lies beyond the gates of ivory; it is a land analogous to the imaginative darkness from which Keats's nightingale sings. It exists on the far side of that Rubicon that Balzac's Eugène de Rastignac must cross if he is to challenge the real world of *Le Père Goriot*. "If there are exceptions to the Draconian laws of the Parisian code, they are to be found in solitude, in men who are never led astray by social doctrines, who live near some clear, fleeting, but ever-running brook . . . happy to listen to the language of the infinite written all about them."[13] As both critics who deplore and critics who applaud the second half of *Lord Jim* agree, Patusan is a romance precinct where, in Hawthorne's words, "actualities would not be so terribly insisted upon."[14] Had "Stein arranged to send [Jim] into a star of the fifth magnitude the change could not have been greater. He left his earthly failings behind him and that sort of reputation he had, and there was a totally new set of conditions for his imaginative faculty to work upon" (p. 218). In Patusan the "straggler yearning inconsolably for his humble place in the ranks" (pp. 224–25) will recreate himself and apply his imaginative gifts to the foundation of an ideal public order. "The conquest of love, honour, men's confidence—the pride of it, the power of it, are fit materials for a heroic tale; only our minds are struck by the externals of such a success, and to Jim's successes there were no externals" (p. 226).

Romance opposes the real history to which realistic fiction is committed; it denies the force of externals. The most heroic conquest of romance would be that of the uncomfortable irony indigenous to the fallen circumstances that realism treats. And Marlow's ambivalence regarding Jim's success in Patusan follows directly from his belief in the necessary work of irony in mediating subjective and objective, ideal meaning and stern fact. Since Marlow's presentation of Jim's case in the first half of the novel opens the way for a fundamental questioning of the premises upon which moral realism rests, it offers the possibility of a new appraisal of the moral status of romance. Jim is no artist. But the compounded self-creation and public creation to which he dedicates himself involve the ideas of selfhood as art and culture as artwork so often treated in early modern fiction. Marlow's reference to the absence of external validation prefaces his divided response and rephrases a traditional realistic reaction to ideal creation. The enigma of art's truth and beauty varies the old conundrum of the cannon fired where no one can hear. Can there be real sound where there are no actual ears? What is the material, the epistemological, and the moral status of imaginative creation? Are Jim and his creation to be regarded as art, illusion, counterfeit, or simply treasonable evasion?

Marlow mistrusts his listeners' willingness and ability to imagine Jim's greatness. But he also distrusts his own willingness. Jim's treason was born in imagination. "There was imagination in that hard skull of his. . . . As to me, I have no imagination (I would be more certain about him to-day, if I had)" (p. 223). Marlow's interest in Jim, he explains, is little more than a passing sentimental curiosity; Jim's fall and his dream make "him touching, just as a man's more intense life makes his death more touching than the death of a tree. I happened to be handy, and I happened to be touched. That's all there is to it" (p. 223). Such words, uttered almost in the same breath as the affirmation of Jim's success, provide the specific terms for the ironies and ambiguities that follow. Marlow speaks with the gruff objectivity of a schoolmaster, a spokesman for the traditional education that moral realism would inculcate, whose lessons risk being compromised by weak sympathy for a wayward pupil. Visiting Jim in Patusan, he is taken aback by the young man's tone. "He was voluble like a youngster on the eve of a long holiday with a prospect of delightful scrapes, and such an attitude of mind in a grown man and in this connection had in it something phenomenal, a little mad, dangerous, unsafe" (p. 234). "This was not a proper frame of mind to approach any undertaking; an improper frame of mind not only for him, I said, but for any man" (p. 236). However, this view, which recalls the traditional generalizing omniscience of the first chapters, is countered by a sense not only of the nature but of the possible truth of youth's imaginative gift. "Youth *is* insolent; it is its right—its necessity; it has got to assert itself, and all assertion in this world of doubts is a defiance, is an insolence" (p. 236).

As the last idea indicates, Marlow's reaction involves much more than the specific case at hand. For Jim's almost lurid intensity of youthful optimism bears on the youth that once marked the world of "us"; the subjective dream is bound up in the heroic glamour that shines in the early days of what is now a staid, profitable, safe, and perhaps hollow moral and material order. The insolence of Jim's undertaking is not so different from the brashness of the seventeenth-century pepper traders who opened up the land to the West and whose exploits Marlow exalts just a few pages earlier. The "bizarre obstinacy of [their] desire made them defy death in a thousand shapes . . . wounds, captivity, hunger, pestilence, and despair. It made them great! By heavens! it made them heroic. . . . It seems impossible to believe that mere greed could hold men to such steadfastness of purpose, to such a blind persistence in endeavor and sacrifice. . . . To us, their less tried successors, they appear magnified, not as agents of trade, but as instruments of a recorded destiny, pushing out into the unknown in obedience to an inward voice, to an impulse beating in the blood, to a dream of the future" (pp. 226–27). Jim's motive is hardly more incredible or unworthy than pepper and greed. By connecting the youth's dream to that of the traders, Marlow includes Patusan in the history of civilization and modifies the romance of Jim's adventure by associating it with the epic enterprises upon the success of which our safe ethos rests. The association suggests a historical and moral content for the dream that Stein conceived as ideal.

Exiled by his crime, arrested in his moral development, Jim moves into an indeterminate realm. The mist that blurs him to Marlow's Western eyes is in part, as Guerard contends, "the aura of deception and self-deception that surrounds Jim's reality."[15] But since Jim's is far more than an "interior" story, the uncertain atmosphere arises from the bafflement of irony as a mature mediating vision. Jim makes romance into a political and moral possibility. His "success" bewilders the traditional ironic premise that youthful dreams must be domesticated and forced to submit to the limits that civil shelter lays down for its protection. When Marlow extols the pepper traders and affirms their greatness and Jim's, he speaks both for the early modern disenchantment with limits and for the adventurous politics spawned by this disenchantment. To the extent that, existentially and culturally, the world no longer conforms to long-established axioms, to the extent we are newly vulnerable in an inimical strangeness, Jim may be an exemplary forerunner of meaningful action. It is this possibility that underlies Marlow's wavering, anxious cogitation about the meaning of Jim's fate in Patusan. Jim looms in uncertainty much as does Kurtz before Marlow meets him. Just as Kurtz is flattered in anticipation by the falseness of the imperial enterprise, so Jim is given stature by the feebleness and hypocrisy of our traditional upbringing. Kurtz tantalizes with the hope of something better than the faithless pilgrims; Jim may be teaching truths unknown in country parsonages. Moreover, unlike Kurtz, Jim sets out to create a civil order. He wants to civilize the "brutes," not to exterminate them.

The atmosphere of Patusan, which confuses real and unreal, material and immaterial, captures uncertainty. Clearly—and it is the only clarity—there is deception. But does the deception arise from Jim, from Marlow, from the nature of things, or from an unaccountable conjunction of all of these? Are we concerned with deception or with the necesary illusion, or even the necessary faith, required by the imposition of moral order? Marlow and Jim watch

(pp. 245-4.6)
> "*the moon float away above the chasm between the hills like an ascending spirit out of a grave; its sheen descended, cold and pale, like the ghost of dead sunlight. There is something haunting in the light of the moon; it has all the dispassionateness of a disembodied soul, and something of its inconceivable mystery. It is to our sunshine, which—say what you like—is all we have to live by, what the echo is to the sound. . . . It robs all forms of matter—which, after all, is our domain—of their substance. . . . The houses . . . vague, grey, silvery forms mingled with black masses of shadow, were like a spectral herd of shapeless creatures pressing forward to drink in a spectral and lifeless stream.*"

The equivocal, suggestive counterpoint between Patusan's echoes of ghostly epic underworlds and Marlow's insistence on the sunlit matter of the order we know creates here and throughout the Patusan narrative a shrouding climate akin to that which Tzvetan Todorov finds in fantasy as a genre. "The fantastic occupies the duration of this uncertainty." "*The reader's hesitation is* . . . the first condition of the fantastic."[16] Conrad, to be sure, is not writing fantasy; at no point does he suggest that Patusan is supernatural. But the effect of the insistent ghostly imagery is to create a symbolic and moral equivalent to the hesitation that Todorov emphasizes.

This hesitation marks Conrad's ambiguous play with his characteristic association of light with order and darkness with the truths and horrors beyond civilization's pale. Amid the gloom of Patusan, "here and there a red gleam twinkled within the bamboo walls, warm, like a living spark, significant of human affections, of shelter, of repose" (p. 246). Jim's efforts fan the spark. At moments he stands as the source of light, dominating "the forest, the secular gloom, the old mankind. He was like a figure set up on a pedestal, to represent in his persistent youth the power, and perhaps the virtues, of races that never grow old, that have emerged from the gloom" (p. 265). The archetypal brightness of youth is magnified morally by the light of the civil order Jim would impose. The beacon of Jim's dream has kindled the hopes of Doramin, the weighty chieftain, and attracted the friendship of his son Dain Waris, one of those rare natives whose virtues resemble our own: "an unobscured vision, a tenacity of purpose, a touch of altruism" (p. 262). Along with community and friendship, Jim's light compels love: the glow of Jim's Jewel. And with Jewel the ideal action and possible moral success of romance near their apogee. Two elements of Jung's triad mount into seeming splendor: the pure hero and his complementary heroine, the anima figure. Yet just as romance action includes a third figure, the bearer of evil that Jung calls shadow, so Jim's luminous endeavor takes place against Marlow's darkling hesitation, against the grim limits of romance creation, and against the nature of real history. "I don't know whether it was exactly fair to him to remember the incident that had given a new direction to his life, but at that very moment I remembered very distinctly. It was like a shadow in the light" (p. 265).

Paradoxically, Jewel, the cynosure of romance, will embody as well the vulnerability that requires all the dull strengths of conventional shelter. When we first hear of her, she seems the perfect reward of dreams. Those in nearby lands, learning the girl's name, believe that Jim has obtained a fabulous gem. "But do you notice how, three hundred miles beyond the end of telegraph cables and mail-boat lines, the haggard utilitarian lies of our civilisation wither and die, to be replaced by pure exercises of imagination, that have the futility, often the charm, and sometimes the deep hidden truthfulness, of works of art? Romance had singled Jim for its own—and that was the true part of the story, which otherwise was all wrong. He did not hide his jewel. In fact, he was extremely proud of it" (p. 282). Conjoining the imaginative truth of pure art with the futility of such truth, Jewel bewilders the premises of Marlow's irony into something approaching incoherence. Women in Conrad not infrequently have this effect: a result of the unstable mixture of romantic idealization and exceptional practical weakness. But Jewel carries both elements to an exemplary extreme. Her love, romance's pure jewel, is also the tragic need that underlies the utilitarian codes and refuges that civil order can provide. She has been maltreated by life. Her stepfather, the petty demon Cornelius, had hounded her mother into death. Jewel, the only witness to her mother's misery, has been nurtured on cruelty and fear. She adores Jim, yet intuits fearfully that she does not fill his heart: that he has a past and a dream that make him unsafe. She fears that he will desert her and that, like her mother, she will "die weeping."

For Marlow, Jewel's dread strikes at the core of Jim's meaning, of his own investment in Jim, and of the irony that our culture enforces. "She should have made for herself a shelter of unexpugnable peace out of that honest affection. She had not the knowledge—not the skill perhaps" (p. 313). With his own doubts about the viability of the order Jim has violated, Marlow too wants to believe that Jim can create a truer shelter. But in Marlow's case knowledge undoes skill. Jewel demands that he affirm, not the greatness of Jim's dream, but its safety. Rhetorically and thematically, her plea intensifies the unbearable necessity for the protection of a lie, a fiction, an illusion, or a faith announced in *Heart of Darkness*.

(p.316) "*Nothing easier than to say, Have no fear! Nothing more difficult. How does one kill fear, I wonder? How do you shoot a spectre through the heart, slash off its spectral head, take it by its spectral*

> throat? It is an enterprise you rush into while you dream, and are glad to make your escape with wet hair and every limb shaking. The bullet is not run, the blade not forged, the man not born; even the winged words of truth drop at your feet like lumps of lead. You require for such a desperate encounter an enchanted and poisoned shaft dipped in a lie too subtle to be found on earth. An enterprise for a dream, my masters!"

Jewel's fear condenses the dread that is the unexpugnable reality of the human situation. It contains the anxiety that brings primal religion or order into being: the "haunting fear that the unaccountable and turbulent powers may at any time bring disaster to human society."[17]

The force of such fear and its truth are the tenor behind Conrad's irony, which is more far-reaching and implacable than that contained in Marlow's ambivalent attitudes. Jim's dream-crafted shelter and the protective illusion that our culture would maintain are both vehicles that distort or conceal or disclaim the fact of fear. Responding to Jewel's need, Marlow tells her that Jim will never leave because he is not good enough to return to the world outside Patusan. But this attempt to rescue truth from the unearthly need for deception cannot assuage the horror of Jewel's pathetic vulnerability. She cries out that Marlow is just repeating the "lie" that Jim has told her. Even Marlow's statement that "nobody, nobody is good enough" (p. 319) is not good enough. "I had only succeeded in adding to her anguish the hint of some mysterious collusion, of an inexplicable and incomprehensible conspiracy to keep her for ever in the dark" (p. 321). Because Marlow believes that our cultural refuge is no less a dream than Jim's creation, he cannot produce the golden bough of faith that might have the absolute force necessary to counter absolute fear. However historically inevitable, his irony serves Jewel no better than Jim's vision.

Yet despite the futility of his encounter with Jewel, Marlow cleaves to the subjective and objective truthfulness that he hopes to find in Jim. Jewel's fear may be the saddest confirmation of pessimism, but her almost worshipful love of Jim may confirm the dream. Hesitation of light and dark, optimism and pessimism, faith and fear continues through the short remainder of Marlow's evening narrative. About to leave the perplexing scene forever, Marlow looks back at Jim alone on the beach. "For me that white figure in the stillness of coast and sea seemed to stand at the heart of a vast enigma. The twilight was ebbing fast . . . he himself appeared no bigger than a child—then only a speck, a tiny white speck, that seemed to catch all the light left in a darkened world" (p. 336). A poignant personal valediction ebbs into a suggestion of cosmic darkness and the questionable public compromises it entails. But the tone of private deprivation dominates: "And suddenly, I lost him . . ." (p. 336; Conrad's ellipsis). For a moment, empathy appears to overrule irony. At the same time, however, a larger perspective than Marlow's is contained in the puzzling echo of Cornelius's attack on Jim a few pages earlier: the intruder who has "stolen" Jewel and upset the gross rule of fear and force is "no more than a little child—a little child" (p. 329). The resonance of youthful possibility is cut off by the suggestion of Jim's childishness. And though Jewel's stepfather is a slimy, greedy outcast, he has a point. So much rhetoric, so much attention, to a child, a simple deserter, a criminal, another outcast?

Marlow's hopes for Jim and for himself through Jim have developed ever further away from the moral bearings so heavily stressed at the beginning. Gradually the account of Jim's fate in Patusan has become in itself the subject of the larger action of ironic hesitation that is *Lord Jim*. Jim's leap, his trial, and his banishment from trust all involve familiar standards; they can be judged against a set of values that provides a firm tenor for a stable moral irony. But the Patusan narrative flirts with an equivocal transmutation of culture's wayward child into the darkling world's only light. Marlow's attitude, to be sure, remains strongly hedged. But Jim is presented as carrying into real history the intemperate absolutism and quixotry that earlier novels of moral realism deem childish and dangerous. The crepuscular imagery comes to seem a means of distancing the implicit heresy in Marlow's view of Jim. The youth's career comes to approximate the subversive plot of the criminal, the rebel against the ranks, or the artist who creates a truer reality than his society can conceive. Jim very nearly creates an identity, a love, a commonweal, and a fate more authentic than those he has left behind. He seems poised to forge on the smithy of boys' books the uncreated conscience of his race.

At this point, however, both narratively and thematically, Marlow's perspective is fractured emphatically. With the introduction of the correspondent to whom Marlow sends the concluding fragments of his tale and the narration of Gentleman Brown within these fragments we enter a complexity that confirms Gérard Genette's comment that the narrative "entanglement reaches the bounds of general intelligibility."[18] As Jim flies in the face of common understanding and truth, and as Marlow unsteadily follows him, we are sternly brought up short by the reported reactions of Marlow's correspondent.

(pp. 338–39)
> "I remember well you would not admit he had mastered his fate. You prophesied for him the disaster of weariness and of disgust with acquired honour, with the self-appointed task, with the love sprung from pity and youth. You had said you knew so well 'that kind of thing,' its illusory satisfaction, its unavoidable deception. You said also . . . that 'giving up your life to them' (them meaning all of mankind with skins brown, yellow, or black, in colour) 'was like selling your soul to a brute.' You contended that 'that kind of thing' was only endurable and enduring when based on a firm conviction in the truth of ideas racially our own, in whose name are established the order, the morality of an ethical progress. . . . 'Without it the sacrifice is only forgetfulness, the way of offering is no better than the way to perdition.' In other words, you maintained that we must fight in the ranks or our lives don't count. Possibly! . . . The point, however, is that of all mankind Jim had no dealings but with himself, and the question is whether at the last he had not confessed to a faith mightier than the laws of order and progress."

The rigid restatement of the code places Marlow's allegiance and the question that underlies it firmly beyond the pale. Jim's faith and Marlow's willingness to entertain it involve a radical separation from the secular religion that ratifies our decency, honor, and truth.

The correspondent's conviction, Marlow's suspension of disbelief, and the near memory of Jewel's dread combine to explain the tremendous stakes involved in Jim's encounter with Gentleman Brown. The enemy Jim confronts is not a "brute" but the perfect perversion of what Marlow calls the "European mind." In Guerard's words, Brown embodies "ruthless and cynical intelligence at the service of pure love of destruction."[19] Brown sails "into Jim's history, a blind accomplice of the Dark Powers" (p. 354). This "man-beast of folklore" (p. 372) is the enigma of evil. The little we learn about him—his possible aristocratic parentage, his fear of confinement, his elopement with a missionary's ailing wife—does nothing to clarify his "complex intention" (p. 353). The information Conrad provides serves only to connect Brown with a tradition of Gothic villains. But to be outside the pale of moral order is to be beyond interpretation; evil is as much the absence of meaning as it is the absence of caritas. Brown is all that opposes civilization. He wields a "blind belief in the righteousness of his will against all mankind, something of that feeling which could induce the leader of a horde of wandering cut-throats to call himself proudly the Scourge of God" (p. 370). Brown's diabolic self-creation opposes the self-appointed faith Jim has been living by. The two face each other as "opposite poles of that conception of life which includes all mankind" (p. 381).

The conflict, "the deadliest kind of duel on which Fate looked on with her cold-eyed knowledge of the end" (p. 385), is, as has been often observed, a brilliantly conceived psychomachia. Schwartz writes that "Gentleman Brown seems to connive with Jim's latent psychic needs to discover the latter's nature and destiny. He presents the lower, darker side that Jim has purged from the world that fulfils his fantasies. Once Jim recognises a mirror image in Gentleman Brown, the social fabric that he has woven on Patusan collapses."[20] Translated into the moral, public terms of an agon involving mankind's conception of itself, the duel has an even more darkly ramified force. For Brown is the nightmare nemesis of all that Jim's dream can represent, the vile secret sharer of Jim's great heresy. The dark "Gentleman" is the horror shadowing the bright "Lord." Brown enacts the reality behind Jewel's dread.

Brown curses Jim as a "hollow sham"; he mocks Jim's "superior soul" (p. 344). Morality, ideals, and high aspirations are lies. Because Brown speaks out of the inscrutable evil that exists in the abyss between our sheltering conception and the factual nature of an alien universe, he shares the equivocal position that Jim himself occupies. Brown's evil is the traditional blackness of melodrama; he is the most nearly perfect figure of evil in Conrad's work. And he is so because he must embody the one truth Jim's dream cannot pass beyond. The only response to Brown would be a version of the landlady's comment on the evil Rigaud in Dickens's *Little Dorrit*: "there are people whom it is necessary to detest without compromise. . . . people who must be dealt with as enemies of the human race . . . people who have no human heart, and who must be crushed like savage beasts and cleared out of the way."[21] To Marlow, meeting Brown later, the man is a vile but shabby demon. But Jim, existing in his shadow land outside fixed meanings, is nakedly vulnerable; he cannot meet evil with the blind conventional conviction for which Dickens's landlady speaks. And Jim's inability takes us back to the conventional wisdom of Marlow's correspondent. Brown's hatred of all order, which he equates with unbearable imprisonment, perversely revises the correspondent's conservatism. Man is fallen; human nature is corruption. The correspondent, like other conservative moralists, responds to the premise by insisting on laws and limits. Those who violate the code invite perdition. But Brown, being perdition incarnate, glories in the premise itself: in our common vileness. He knows that Jim's story "is no better than mine. I've lived—and so did you though you talk as if you were one of those people that should have wings so as to go about without touching the dirty earth. Well—it is dirty. I haven't got any wings. I am here because I was afraid once in my life. . . . I won't ask you what scared you into this infernal hole" (p. 383). "And there ran through the rough talk a vein of subtle reference to their common blood, an assumption of common experience; a sickening suggestion of common guilt, of secret knowledge that was like a bond of their minds and of their hearts" (p. 387). In their opposing ways, both men do share the knowledge that "nobody is good enough." Brown glories in the fact; Jim would overleap the fact. But the fact is what necessitates the moral order of civilization's ranks; it is at the core of Jewel's dread; it is the gravest argument against Jim's dream of creating a better order out of and by himself.

The truth mightier than we know, which is the hope Marlow invests in the dream, carries with it the refusal of traditional doubts about man's ability to create order out of his weak or fallen nature. The public consequences of Jim's sanguine faith seem to reinforce the traditional worldly irony that Marlow's account has been trying to sidestep. For Jim is no longer alone in his dream. With him are Jewel, Dain Waris, and the entire "social fabric of orderly, peaceful life, when every man was sure of to-morrow, the edifice raised by Jim's hands" (p. 373). Jim advises that Brown be allowed to depart in peace. The natives are shocked, but "most of them simply said that they 'believed Tuan Jim.'"

> "In this simple form of assent to his will lies the whole gist of the situation; their creed, his truth; and the testimony to that faithfulness which made him in his own eyes the equal of the impeccable men who never fall out of the ranks. Stein's words, 'Romantic!—Romantic!' seem to ring over those distances that will never give him up now to a world indifferent to his failings and virtues, and to that ardent and clinging affection [Jewel's love] that refuses him the dole of tears in the bewilderment of a great grief and of eternal separation. From the moment the sheer truthfulness of his last three years of life carries the day against the ignorance, the fear, and the anger of men, he appears no longer to me as I saw him last—a white speck catching all the dim light left upon a sombre coast and the darkened sea—but greater and more pitiful in the loneliness of his soul, that remains even for her who loved him best a cruel and insoluble mystery."

(p. 393)

Jim's last acts in Patusan sharply delimit the greatness that Marlow continues to affirm. Jim and Brown exchange promises of mutual forbearance. "It is evident that he did not mistrust Brown"; Jim could not know "the almost inconceivable egotism of the man which made him, when resisted and foiled in his will, mad with the indignant and revengeful rage of a thwarted autocrat" (p. 394). Because Jim cannot know, Dain Waris and others are killed; the social edifice collapses. "We shall have to fight," Jim's faithful servant tells him. "'Fight! What for?' he asked. 'For our lives.' 'I have no life,' he said" (p. 409). Leaving Jewel and the others who still believe in him behind, Jim goes to stand before Dain Waris's father; he takes full responsibility for the disaster and allows himself to be shot. Neither the misjudgment nor the romantic egoism of this final gesture denies Jim's truthfulness. But if trust in the shelter his creed would raise up is the gist of the situation, then Jim's individual truth and faithfulness are beside the point. However great, however pitiful in the spotlight of his mysterious isolation, Jim has again failed. No man alone can achieve the safety that is the truth and grand illusion of our moral Realpolitik. Yet despite this strong implication, Marlow's final estimate is still hesitant.

> "And that's the end. He passes away under a cloud, inscrutable at heart, forgotten, unforgiven, and excessively romantic. Not in the wildest days of his boyish visions could he have seen the alluring shape of such an extraordinary success! For it may very well be that in the short moment of his last proud and unflinching glance, he had beheld the face of that opportunity which, like an Eastern bride, had come veiled to his side.
>
> (p. 416) "But we can see him, an obscure conqueror of fame, tearing himself out of the arms of a jealous love at the sign, at the call of his exalted egoism. He goes away from a living woman to celebrate his pitiless wedding with a shadowy ideal of conduct. . . . Now he is no more, there are days when the reality of his existence comes to me with an immense, with an overwhelming force; and yet upon my honour there are moments, too, when he passes from my eyes like a disembodied spirit astray amongst the passions of this earth, ready to surrender himself faithfully to the claims of his own world of shades."

To the end, Marlow is torn between the two conceptions of meaning through which he views Jim. Moving upriver into Patusan, Jim has passed beyond clear vision and through the gates of dream. For the French lieutenant or Marlow's correspondent, and often for Marlow himself, the gates are of ivory: the portal to false prophecy and deluding vision. The irony founded upon "the morality of an ethical progress" casts Jim as preposterously childish, as unreal. The issues raised by Jim's story pertain only to the world of shades. For the romantic idealist Stein and by extension for the modern tradition that would revise naive romantic individualism into the art of self-creation, the gates may be those of horn: the entry to true dreams. For the Marlow that affirms Jim's success, Jim's ideal follows the splendid will-o'-the-wisp of imaginative reality; the dream courts all the glamour, brightness, and intensity that should attend man's moral enterprise. This idea of Jim is no less shrouded in irony than the former, but the irony is of a different kind. For Marlow's imaginative empathy and the subjective allegiance that accompanies it construe Jim's endeavor, not as a delusion or a lie, but as something resembling a fiction, an artwork. And the irony here is similar to romantic irony: a moral and epistemological self-consciousness about the reality of what imagination can create: a questioning of the relation between the truths of facts and the truths of spirit.

Marlow's flickering hope that the "obscure truth" of Jim's mystery may be "momentous enough to affect mankind's conception of itself" gives life to his narrative. But Marlow is himself always at least half-aware of a larger perspective: that of the novel's irony in regard to private dreams. For in *Lord Jim* Conrad places Marlow's hope for Jim in much the same ironic distance as that Marlow himself employs to convey Jim's dedication to his ideal yet spectral success. Jim's story is paired with Marlow's empathic account of the story's momentousness; both become part of a rueful, ironic valediction to romantic aspiration. Speaking biographically, we may hazard as others have done that Conrad is turning from his romantic father's spirit to accept the lessons of necessity and futility that his practical uncle would teach. Speaking more directly to Conrad's themes as they will develop from *Lord Jim* to *Under Western Eyes*, we can say that Conrad's attitudes are already more somber and more ironic than Marlow's hesitations. That Marlow embodies much of his creator's commitment to the reality of ambiguity is evident. And part of Conrad may be as romantic as Jim and as attuned to romance as Marlow. But Conrad's own conception of romance has left the individual instance behind;

the concerns evident in the nakedness of the *Patna* pilgrims adrift in a cruel universe, in Jewel's dread, and in Gentleman Brown's evil demand what is usually termed a political perspective. The individual's dreamwork, even though it involves the creation of moral order, elicits less of Conrad's interest than the necessities and ironies of the momentous illusion-making that is vested in the idea of civilization. In the progress of Conrad's concerns, the still personal scorn and duality with which Marlow regards our shelter of words will lead to the perplexing public meaning accorded the Western language teacher who narrates *Under Western Eyes*; the vulnerable pilgrims, the fearful girl, and the fact of evil will comingle in the appalling mystery that is Russia.

Jim's dream is not so much rejected as it is passed beyond. The last lines of the novel leave Jewel trailing out "a soundless, inert life in Stein's house." Stein himself, the mentor of romantic idealism, has aged markedly; he is preparing for death, and in the final words of the narrative "waves his hand sadly at his butterflies" (pp. 416–17). A page earlier, in his parting comment on Jim, Marlow seems willing to subordinate the pathos of the living woman to the glamour of the Eastern bride, the consort of Jim's dream. But the concluding scene joins Jewel to the Intended, Emilia Gould, and Winnie Verloc as a symbol, however chauvinistic on Conrad's part, of the purity, fidelity, and frailty of women: an embodiment of values and needs that demand a more responsible fiction than Jim's. And with whatever ambivalence and regret, it is to this objective fiction, to the politics of illusion, that Conrad turns in his next novel.

II

NOSTROMO
The Irony of Faithful Service

EACH OF CONRAD'S FOUR MAJOR NOVELS juxtaposes an unexceptional protagonist against the complex and equivocal irony that is the key signature of all human endeavor. Jim's dream is the stuff of popular romance; his fate involves the nature of private desiring, the validity of culture, and the reality of evil. Winnie Verloc, a flat descendant of Mrs. Micawber, places in simple doubt the faith in a safe but limited lot that underlies moral realism. Razumov, a bright, sensitive, lonely young man, wants no more than to be a recognized cog in the service of his state; but his desire for simple normality leads him into a story that would challenge the most heroic of tragic overreachers. In *Nostromo*, the inimitable Capataz de Cargadores, Gian' Battista Fidanza, whom Edward Said terms "the quintessential man of action," provides the simple pivot around which swirl the ironies of the dream of moral statecraft.[1] The four characters are, of course, markedly different, but each varies the situation employed repeatedly in the fictions of naturalism: the unleashing upon an average person of the cosmic forces and ironies associated with late-century pessimism. In Conrad's novels this confrontation inevitably takes the shape of an investigation of the possibility for a sheltering and morally truthful faith in civil order.

Gian' Battista acts effectively and gloriously to serve the dream of an Occidental republic in Sulaco. He is as crucial a resource as the San Tomé silver—indeed, Schwartz refers to him as the "silver metamorphosed."[2] His "inspiriting" leadership forges "an outcast lot of very mixed blood" into efficient service (pp. 14–15). With splendid brio he rescues President Ribiera, saves the threatened treasure, and dashes across country to bring back General Barrios and his guns in time to quell Montero. Those whom the Capataz serves have every reason to dub him Nostromo, our man. In all senses—material, Marxist, moral—he is a value. Repeatedly, he carries forward the banner of progress that the British chairman of the railway and his chief engineer see in the link they are constructing between Sulaco and the inland capital. The enterpise will generate "a power for the world's service—a subtle force that could set in motion mighty machines, men's muscles, and awaken also in human breasts an unbounded devotion to the task. . . . the force would be almost as strong as a faith. Not quite, however" (p. 41). Nostromo is the foreman of this near-faith and of the irony that surrounds it.

In himself, the Capataz is luminously uncomplicated. He is so purely without shadow as to seem contentless. Conrad feared that he might be too vacant a creation. Writing to Cunninghame Graham shortly after the novel's publication, he allowed that "truly N. is nothing at all—a fiction, embodied vanity of the sailor kind—a romantic mouthpiece of the 'people.'"[3] The fiction, however, is wonderfully attractive. It conveys at times the "beautiful, unspoiled freedom" that Said finds in the "splendidly theatrical moment" when Nostromo sheers off his silver buttons to appease his sweetheart.[4] The Capataz achieves the perfect glory of pristine action. No doubt, as we are told in reference to Charles Gould's dream of reopening the mine that had defeated his father: "Action is consolatory. It is the enemy of thought and the friend of flattering illusions" (p. 66). But while the illusions of other major characters are intricate, Nostromo's is not. He requires only that his deeds be rewarded with the public acclaim that feeds his vanity. This vanity is his identity. His fiction is an all-engrossing present tense; his private life is his public action. He is a primitive, a throwback to the unselfconscious epoch that Schiller terms the naive. The other characters belong to the modern skeptical age in which thought, sentiment, and action are dissociated. Even the good-natured simpleton Captain Mitchell feels twinges of complex compunction and guilt. Nostromo springs from a realm in which all the motions of the psyche find external expression. He seems to have stepped out of the epic cultures inhabited by Gogol's Taras Bulba, Tolstoy's Hadji Murad, and Conrad's own Gaspar Ruiz.

But Gian' Battista has stepped out; he is no part of the devoted world of epic wholeness. He has forsworn his sailor's service to "come ashore casually to try his luck in Costaguana" (p. 130). Though he has succeeded brilliantly, his vanity is not quite an equivalent to the spiritual integrity that sophisticated writers so often idealize in an epic past. Nostalgia is no part of Conrad's theme. What Captain Mitchell calls Nostromo's "force of character" (p. 13) is dependent on the force generated by the dream of moral civilization. As the proud discoverer and employer of the Capataz, Mitchell resembles the chief accountant whom Marlow praises in *Heart of Darkness*. In "the great demoralization of the land he kept up his appearance. . . . His starched collars and got-up shirt-fronts were achievements of character. . . . I could not help asking him how he managed to sport such linen. He had just the faintest blush, and said modestly, 'I've been teaching one of the native women about the station. It was difficult. She had a distaste for the work.' Thus this man had verily accomplished something" (p. 68). Given the cosmic irony of demoralization, the accountant's efforts are moral achievements. But Marlow's sardonic tone implies that the achievement is both somewhat ludicrous in itself and equivocal in relation to the native. The accountant conforms to an ironic necessity; his conformity is made the butt of a different irony; the two ironies—those of admirable shelter and of scorn for such got-up shelter—combine to baffle judgment. Sulaco is a far cry from the African station; but the Captain and the Capataz are contained within an ironic perspective not unlike that in which Marlow views the accountant and the native woman. Mitchell is the admirable speciousness of moral order in an alien world; Nostromo is the creature of this order.

Gian' Battista joins the primitive gifts of the "people" to the valuable force of the proletariat. His energy is the raw material of effective civilization. He is a special and exemplary test case for the point that Robert Penn Warren makes in implying that the material order provided by the mine provides the peon-workers with a purpose and a safety quite absent from their home in the Campo.[5] If the state that derives its being from the mine is to fulfill what Emilia Gould terms its "justificative conception" (p. 107), if it is to become "a rallying point for everything in the province that needed order and stability to live" (p. 110), then the amoral resource of a Nostromo must be invested with something like the "force of faith" and "stern devotion to a cause" (p. 31) that guide Giorgio Viola, the Garabaldino in exile. Egotistic vanity must be transformed into the pride of true devotion. In himself, Gian' Battista is a figure of "helpless strength" (p. 420). Just as the silver must be refined into moral statecraft, so he must be endowed with the strength of ethical meaning and purpose that Victorian moral realism enshrines in its idea of character.

Nostromo, of course, as almost all readers and critics agree, is a radically skeptical work. The moral imperatives that the Capataz, the silver, and the state ought to fulfill are debased. Yet these public dreams define the framework for the irony that Nostromo lives out. The civil, ethical identity with which "our man" is associated at the beginning collapses into the personal, domestic pathos of theft and seduction with which the novel concludes. Guerard and others are right in viewing this ending as less than successful narratively and rhetorically. Conrad's treatments of merely private life, whatever their thematic function, tend to be weak. But the weakness in this novel can only be viewed as providing yet another irony. Nostromo, reduced at last to the uninspired and inefficient Captain Fidanza, is indeed what Guerard calls the "lost subject" of the book.[6] He is so, however, in an intentionally ironic as well as an unintentionally aesthetic sense. The republic of which the Goulds and their associates dream is equally the novel's lost subject. When Nostromo's occupation is lost, when the Capataz swims back to Azuera to be reborn as simple Gian' Battista, he becomes the register of the novel's ironic understanding of irony itself. Both in its service and in its decline into the commonplace romance of Captain Fidanza's last months, Nostromo's "genius" mirrors the irony that mocks and protects Emilia Gould's love, hope, and sacrifice.

The transformation of Gian' Battista into Nostromo, the emergence of a public title out of a private name, promises a more hopeful drama. No doubt, as Said observes, the use of flattering appositional phrases to exalt Nostromo is excessive,[7] but the title belongs among those abundant tags and nicknames in Conrad's fiction that extend individuality into a larger communal reference. As Captain Lingard tells Mrs. Travers in *The Rescue*: "I am King Tom, Rajah Laut, and fit to look any man hereabouts in the face. I have my name to take care of. Everything rests on that." Mrs. Travers replies that the Spanish "would express this by saying that everything rests on honour" (p. 291). Gian' Battista is by no means alone in associating his private value with the prestige conferred by the cognomen that provides the novel's title. "A nickname," the chief engineer tells Decoud, "may be the best record of a success" (p. 316). The engineer, who is explaining why Charles Gould is called "El Rey de Sulaco," goes on to comment: "That's what I call putting the face of a joke upon the body of a truth." But no more than in *Lord Jim* is the relation between a title and a truth a simple joke. The discrepancy between name and thing belongs to the black humor of cosmic irony. Naming involves the ironies of the fiction through which mankind would create meaning and protection. As Giorgio Viola's wife bitterly observes, Nostromo corrupts true Italian (p. 23); the tag should be *nostr'uomo*. The possessive compounds with a truncated noun to announce the flawed conjunction of public and private realms, of illusion and raw material.

What the mine is to Charles Gould, the prestige of his nickname is to Nostromo. Schwartz comments that when "Nostromo gradually drifts into bondage to the treasure, he becomes Gould's double."[8] But the ironic counterpoint is implicit from the beginning. Gould's dedication to San Tomé is a sophisticated and self-conscious variation upon the Capataz's naive vanity. Gian' Battista "looks upon his prestige as a sort of investment," while at the same time prizing "it for its own sake" (pp. 220–21). Just as Gould draws sustenance from the republicans and from Holroyd, so Nostromo finds his fortune and his identity in "the adulation of the common people and the confidence of his superiors" (p. 226). Of course, the Capataz is a simple man of action, far inferior to those who conceive the new republic. The Goulds, Holroyd, Don José Avellanos, and their supporters are the power that dreams the state into being. Nostromo is the efficient midwife, the "active usher-in of the material implements for our progress" as Decoud puts it (p. 191).

The dream depends on its man; the man mines the dream for the treasure, the honor, that supports his self-esteem.

For most of the novel Nostromo's role is little more than a projection of his splendid efficiency. Like Beaumarchais's Figaro and his operatic namesakes, the Capataz overcomes practical obstacles and forwards his masters' dreams. Unlike Figaro, who is sardonically aware of the class value of his prowess and of the tinsel hollowness of his superiors, Gian' Battista has no depth of consciousness. What we know of him comes mainly from the patronizing speculations of Decoud, Dr. Monygham, and others. He is illustrational, not representational. His dependence on the settings, circumstances, and interests of the novel's organizing concerns makes him an example of the equation between character and thematic environment postulated in recent narrative theory.[9] Indeed, his pathetic fall from dependence into an independence of being he cannot manage provides a provocative footnote to the theoretical premise. The Capataz seems almost to wish to avoid the responsibility of character. Schwartz, stressing the importance of family values, notes that Giorgio and Teresa Viola incorporate Gian' Battista into their lives as a surrogate for their dead son.[10] But most of Nostromo's efforts are directed at keeping clear of the emotional ties such a connection entails. He wants no private life; his being is his deeds. And since private life in the novel is always in a state of frustrating thralldom to public dreams, his refusal seems understandable. Though related to the flat victims of Conrad's earlier novels, he anticipates Winnie Verloc's unwillingness to look deeply into herself or into life as well as Razumov's craving for a wholly serviceable existence.

Nostromo's absorption in his own glamour sets him off from the Congo natives, *Patna* pilgrims, and Jewel. On the spectrum of betrayals at the core of Conrad's major fiction he occupies a position between naked victimization and ambiguous accountability. Not only Decoud and Dr. Monygham but the narrative voice as well treat the theatrical egotism of the Capataz's simplicity with condescension. "Like other men of southern races in whom the complexity of simple conceptions is much more apparent than real," he is "as ready to become the prey of any belief, superstition, or desire as a child" (ML, p. 466).[11] As an embodiment and spokesman for the "popular mind" (p. 420), Gian' Battista is far from the ideal that Conrad invests in simple seamen such as Singleton; just as he is set below the austere, devoted Garabaldino, so he has no share in the "inborn and subtle and everlasting" dedication, that "something solid like a principle, and masterful like an instinct," which Marlow cherishes in his English seamates in "Youth" (p. 28). In jumping ship to gratify his vanity ashore, he recalls the deplorable Willems in *An Outcast of the Islands*, who rejects the spirit of true seamanship out of "an instinctive contempt for the honest simplicity of that work which led to nothing he cared for" (p. 17). To be sure, Nostromo's splendid service outshines his deficiencies. But these limitations, being those of the "people" who support and are supported by the state, become one of the novel's most extensive sources of irony. When Nostromo's public occupation is ended, when he can no longer be "our man" but must create himself from his own resources, the impurity of his metal will doom him.

In no sense does Gian' Battista's nature doom the dream as well. But because the Capataz is what he is, because like the silver itself he is an intrinsically neutral, amoral resource, his qualities become an ironic counterweight to Emilia Gould's vision of an ideal order. Human, political, and cosmic flaws turn Emilia's "imaginative estimate" of the silver's moral power into irony. She would endow the "metal with a justificative conception, as though it were not a mere fact, but something far-reaching and impalpable, like the true expression of an emotion or the emergence of a principle" (p. 107). Nostromo's mere factuality is as resistant to such idealistic alchemy as the silver. Emilia's dream combines the idea of legendary treasure with the potential for poetic statecraft that Goethe in *Wilhelm Meister* and German romantic writers such as Novalis associate with earth's subterranean bounty. Yet from the initial reference to the lost gringo treasure hunters haunting the Azuera with their greed, the dream is shadowed by the irony of the demonic force of material interests. Nostromo compounds this public or even general irony with the moral inertness of his popular nature. The fact that so high a goal depends on so limited a creature is deflating. And this situational irony involves a broader, more bitter truth—one with which Conrad's fiction becomes ever more darkly involved. The moral community of shelter, decency, fidelity, and faith that Conrad's best characters work to maintain is not a bright haven of culture but a bulwark for the likes of Gian' Battista. The ironic potential of this recognition develops from Nostromo to the flat Londoners in *The Secret Agent* and the complacent Genevans in *Under Western Eyes*.

Yet the account of Gian' Battista's decline from the service of the state to the pursuit of self-interest that dominates the final quarter of the novel emphasizes pathetic waste rather than human hollowness. The squandering of the man's public value and the loss of his occupation counterpoint the bitter frustration that is Emilia's fate. Both sadnesses are encased in the irony that grows out of the inefficiency of the fictions in which mankind seeks shelter and meaning. With his vanity defrauded and his world undone, Nostromo is thrown back on his own invention. And this invention bears the hopes and insufficiencies of a popular mind cast adrift in an alien set of circumstances. The Capataz's all-engrossing and rewarding service has been his faith. Now he must create a faith.

During his urgent preparations for the desperate enterprise of spiriting the silver out of Montero's reach, Nostromo learns that Teresa Viola is dangerously ill. He takes time to find a doctor, but refuses to seek about for a priest. Later, hearing of her death, he utters "the pious formula" of the people—"May God have her soul!"—"from the superficial force of habit, but with a deep-seated sincerity." The passage that follows, which is as far from Mitchell's flatulent praise as it is from Decoud's skepticism, provides the thematic premise for Gian' Battista's attempt at self-creation.

(p. 420)
> *The popular mind is incapable of scepticism; and that incapacity delivers their helpless strength to the wiles of swindlers and to the pitiless enthusiasms of leaders inspired by visions of a high destiny. . . . His scorn of priests as priests remained; but after all, it was impossible to know whether what they affirmed was not true. Power, punishment, pardon, are simple and credible notions. The magnificent Capataz de Cargadores, deprived of certain simple realities, such as the admiration of women, the adulation of men,*

> the admired publicity of his life, was ready to feel the burden of
> sacrilegious guilt descend upon his shoulders.

The helpless force of the people requires the moral and civil power "almost as strong as a faith" that is for Conrad the burden and achievement of civilization. As in Marlow's comments on Jewel, the narrative of Gian' Battista's plight mixes pained empathy, belittlement, and ambiguous patterns of blame. The Capataz is a victim of his own primitive consciousness and of the incapacity—whether culpable or inevitable—of statecraft to supply the shelter and direction of a traditional faith. One may speak, as Said does, of Nostromo's accession "to the role of principal hero."[12] But the emphasis is on the shame and waste implicit in this development. Nostromo's inability to create a self that might function appropriately and meaningfully in the embattled world of cross-purposes portrayed in Costaguana and Sulaco is as bleak, incongruous, and ironic a human fact as Jewel's or Winnie Verloc's feminine vulnerability. Jewel looks to Jim for the simple reality of faithful protection; Winnie believes in her husband. In both women the ironic betrayal is more real than the kind of faith betrayed. With Nostromo, the situation is similar, but the stakes are more fearfully exemplary. For beyond the human actors and their entanglements lies the dream of civil order itself. Gian' Battista is not betrayed by one person's dream or another's limitations; he is cast down by the seemingly unavoidable failure of a human political and moral fiction.

At the beginning of Nostromo's desperate effort to save the silver, the material treasure is entrusted to the human treasure. Along with the bemused and skeptical Decoud, the Capataz steers the lighterload of ingots out into the darkness of the Gulfo Placido. The confidence of his superiors is so complete that few words need to be spoken. Then, for several days, nothing is heard. The silence of trust becomes a dumbness. The silver has been saved from Montero, but Nostromo and Decoud are presumed to be lost. Yet against the odds, the enterprise has succeeded. The treasure is stashed on the Great Isabel, the largest island in the gulf; Decoud has been left on the island to prepare for his further mission; Nostromo, after jettisoning the lighter, has swum back to shore. Reasonably enough, he expects praise for his achievement; he craves the light of recognition that will, after so much silence and obscurity, replenish the special brightness that is his vanity and his identity. Instead, he enters an empty port and encounters Dr. Monygham who scoffs at him and his success.

For the return is the dark side of the setting out. Publicity sours into baffling secrecy. When Nostromo crawls from the water onto the shore of Azuera, that deserted peninsula supposedly haunted by the gringo treasure hunters, he emerges stripped of himself. He surfaces "with the lost air of a man just born into the world." Falling into a deathlike sleep, he awakens "as natural and free from evil . . . as a magnificent and unconscious wild beast" (pp. 411–12). Slowly he regains "his hold on the world." Just before embarking with the silver, he had given his last dollar to an old woman grief-stricken at the disappearance of her son. "Performed in obscurity and without witnesses," the act

(p. 414) *had still the characteristics of splendour and publicity, and was in strict keeping with his reputation. But this awakening in solitude, except for the watchful vulture, amongst the ruins of the fort, had no such characteristics. His first confused feeling was exactly this—that it was not in keeping. It was more like the end of things. The necessity of living concealed somehow, for God knows how long, which assailed him on his return to consciousness, made everything that had gone before for years appear vain and foolish, like a flattering dream come suddenly to an end.*

With a consciousness no greater than that needed to savor his reputation, Gian' Battista is thrust into the realm of interlocking duplicities and ironies in which Conrad's next two novels will be set. "Each man must have some temperamental sense by which to discover himself. With Nostromo it was vanity of an artless sort. Without it he would have been nothing. It called out his recklessness, his industry, his ingenuity" (ML, p. 461). Such simplicity is no preparation for the psychological drama now to begin. Nostromo is even less suited for the intangibilities of a self-generated reality than Winnie Verloc. His facile egotism begins to crumble at the thought of a life eked out in secrecy. "The confused and intimate impressions of universal dissolution which beset a subjective nature at any strong check to its ruling passion had a bitterness approaching that of death itself. And no wonder—with no intellectual existence or moral strain to carry on his individuality, unscathed, over the abyss left by the collapse of his vanity; for even that had been simply sensuous and picturesque, and could not exist apart from outward show" (ML, p. 466).

To become Nostromo, Gian' Battista has been willing to postpone immediate gratifications for the sake of the accolades lavished on his service. At the time when he sets out to save the silver he has achieved a simple version of the balance between material and sensuous desires and higher purposes that for Conrad validates moral imperialism. Nostromo's ego is the register and reward of the republic his superiors would create. His character is a true accomplishment of the dream, but it is also part of the dream. When the dream ends, splendor, hope, and accomplishment all collapse into embittered irony. The sardonic Dr. Monygham, who sees the hollowness of material statecraft and the shallowness of Gian' Battista, will take over from those who have dreamed Nostromo into being. The ugly doctor with his "evil reputation" (p. 410) will, of course, save the foundering republic. But for Gian' Battista the doctor's reality simply confirms the bad faith and betrayal into which he has awakened. "His imagination had seized upon the clear and simple notion of betrayal to account for the dazed feeling of enlightenment as to being done for, of having inadvertently gone out of his existence on an issue in which his personality had not been taken into account. A man betrayed is a man destroyed" (pp. 419–20).

Dr. Monygham's skepticism presides over the reversion of Nostromo into the components of primitive superstition, class animus, and egocentric desire that had been alchemized in the Capataz's public value. The outward show becomes ironic spectacle. Just as Captain Mitchell will lavish his fulsome praise of the new republic's sunny material conveniences against the background of Charles Gould's moral treason, Emilia's desolation, and the hollowness of the young state, so Gian' Battista will once again perform his splendid service. But the spirit that gave meaning to his inimitable fidelity is destroyed. Previously, he listened to Giorgio Viola's fervid revolutionist comments and to Teresa's bitter populist scorn with indifference. Now he mouths their words as expressions of his conviction of betrayal and dedication to vengeance. He has been treated as the fine people's dog. The power he served is without authority; he must bear the shame for letting Teresa die without a priest. "In the downfall of all the realities that made his force, he was affected by . . . superstition" (p. 418). Wandering lost and angry about the docks that were once his kingdom, he meets Dr. Monygham whom he dislikes and distrusts. But the doctor's disenchantment with all human illusions is now gratifying. In his small way, Nostromo has been denuded of himself much as Dr. Monygham was when tortured by the tyrant Guzman Bento. No longer does the doctor seem a futile nay-sayer; his mocking truthtelling seems as reliable to Gian' Battista as it does to the reader. "None of your friends could reward you and protect you just now, Capataz. Not even Don Carlos [Gould] himself." The only chance to recapture his character is in another desperate enterprise. "The choice was between accepting the mission to Barrios, with all its dangers and difficulties, and leaving Sulaco by stealth, ingloriously, in poverty" (p. 455).

Between a meaningless dream and a naked nightmare there is little to choose. In his perilous, lonely venture to save the silver Nostromo had been shielded by his faith that his superiors would reward his value. Now he acts in a void and is preyed upon by mistrust and disbelief. Narrative omniscience is withdrawn from his service and refocused on Dr. Monygham's. The mission takes place offstage. After the doctor convinces him that he must go, he hides out briefly with Giorgio Viola. Overcome by Teresa's death, the Garabaldino is friendly, but self-absorbed. "Nostromo saw clearly that the old man understood nothing of the words. There was no one to understand; no one he could take into the confidence of Decoud's fate, of his own, into the secret of the silver" (p. 469). "He could only hold his tongue, since there was no one to trust" (p. 471).

The hopeful vision that the chairman of railways announces and the brightness that Mitchell advertises have been cast into dark decline. But the action recounted in the last sections of the novel is governed by irony, not horror. On his mission to bring back the general and the guns Nostromo serves Dr. Monygham; the doctor, in "the fanaticism of his devotion, fed on the sense of his abasement" (p. 453), serves the one truth in his broken life: Emilia Gould. Yet the goddess is now almost powerless. The hope has shrunk to a stricken sense of pathos. The doctor is no believer in the theatrical publicity the Capataz craves, but he does believe in Nostromo's special prowess. "He esteemed highly the intrepidity of that man, whom he valued but little, being disillusioned as to mankind in general, because of the particular instance in which his own manhood had failed" (p. 433). In his own version of the admiration of embattled sophistication for invincible primitivism, Dr. Monygham is "eminently fit to appreciate" the Capataz's successful encounter with solitude. Nostromo's ingenuous egotism, the doctor believes, saved him from "the crushing, paralyzing sense of human littleness, which is what really defeats a man . . . alone, far from the eyes of his fellows" (p. 433). Only Nostromo can save what little remains of the dream. He must be persuaded to do so by an appeal to his egotism. And this appeal, which launches the Capataz into the blankness he abhors, involves another of those lies that figure so centrally in Conrad's irony.

The craven Hirsch has been killed by Sotillo, Montero's greedy officer who for the moment controls the port. Dr. Monygham knows that the death and Sotillo's motives are all-important. But he is baffled. To prod Nostromo into action, he must pretend to omniscience. He is willing to sacrifice himself for Emilia Gould's sake. "To lie, to deceive, to circumvent even the basest of mankind was odious to him. . . . He had made that sacrifice in a spirit of abasement. He had said to himself bitterly, 'I am the only one fit for that dirty work.' And he believed this. He was not subtle. His simplicity was such that, though he had no sort of heroic idea of seeking death, the risk, deadly enough, to which he exposed himself, had a sustaining and comforting effect. To that spiritual state the fate of Hirsch presented itself as part of the general atrocity of things" (p. 439). Whereas Marlow's lies to the Intended and to Jewel are justified by the redeeming truth of moral and civic shelter, Dr.

Monygham lies on behalf of a cause in which he cannot believe and a woman whose ideal truth is of no avail. Dr. Monygham's words do awaken "the genius of that Genoese seaman which dominated the destinies of great enterprises and of many people, the fortunes of Charles Gould, the fate of an admirable woman" (p. 452). But Nostromo's genius is now a reflex of desperate bewilderment, anger, and starved egotism. The doctor's own skepticism is as simplistically absolute as the Capataz's vanity. The general atrocity of the situation is far from the glamorous rhetoric of Marlow's response to Jewel's plight: "You require for such a desperate encounter an enchanted and poisoned shaft dipped in a lie too subtle to be found on earth." Dr Monygham is not subtle; his response to the challenge of his devotion to Emilia's compromised truth is the lowest denominator of what was in Conrad's earlier fiction a high faith. The dramatic hesitation of *Heart of Darkness* and *Lord Jim*, the heroic tension between the fictive yet real achievement of civilization and the stark encounter with the horror beyond our pale, give way to an ironic minimalism. The fiction of civilization is becoming a dirty work: often distasteful and sometimes vulgar, involving sustenance and comfort rather than moral purpose. Dr. Monygham's deceit announces the theme of violated service that dominates the remainder of *Nostromo*. At the same time, however, the doctor's bitter devotion, Gian' Battista's betrayed genius, and Emilia's squandered truth are all presented as containing an irreducible modicum of value. If anything, the debasement and simple need are the ingredients of a less appealing but truer faith than the fine ethical art that Emilia—and Conrad—once trusted in. The irony of Conrad's next novels will depend upon this ungainly conjunction of abased vehicles and minimal faith. The service that Dr. Monygham convinces Nostromo to undertake anticipates the stolid truth of the London crowds in *The Secret Agent*: however brutalized and suspect its motives, it provides real protection.

The dash to bring back Barrios succeeds. But betrayal, mystery, and mistrust transform public agency into ambiguous, secret service. Decoud has not been heard of; his fate, after having been left alone with the silver that he and Gian' Battista had hidden on Great Isabel, is unknown. Dark perplexities dim the pure light that would satisfy Nostromo's vanity. To gain answers he leaps overboard from the general's ship as it sails toward the port and swims to the island. He is appalled to discover that some of the treasure is missing.

(pp. 502–3)
> *And four ingots! Did [Decoud] take them in revenge, to cast a spell, like the angry [Teresa] who had prophesied remorse and failure, and yet had laid upon him the task of saving the children? Well, he had saved the children. He had defeated the spell of poverty and starvation. He had done it all alone—or perhaps helped by the devil. Who cared? He had done it, betrayed as he was, and saving by the same stroke the San Tomé mine, which appeared to him hateful and immense, lording it by its vast wealth over the valour, the toil, the fidelity of the poor, over war and peace, over the labours of the town, the sea, and the Campo.*

The violation of the treasure, like the betrayal of his own value, appears to confirm a general conspiracy. Gian' Battista in his simplicity jumbles his superstitious fear of dark powers with a naive awareness of economic oppression. Yet his conviction of inexplicable victimization leads, not to a paralysis, but to an altered belief in the nature and power of his genius. The vanity of outward show with its power to serve his superiors and their dream gives way to unabashed selfish materialism. "I must grow rich very slowly," he concludes (p. 503). The bravura, epic resource of inimitable service, the treasure that has just rescued the state, reverts from public fidelity to private gratification. The civil cognomen, Nostromo, is to become only an irony.

The Capataz's cynicism registers the erosion of moral meaning that accompanies the success of material interests. The atmosphere of falling off darkens the Campo, the new republic, and the gulf. But Gian' Battista's moral decline must be set against the belated narrative of the fate of his companion in the desperate enterprise. Through rhetorical and thematic parallels and juxtapostions, Decoud's suicide is inextricably bound into Nostromo's corrupted service. Though Gian' Battista never learns what has happened to the skeptical patriot and the four ingots, the account of Decoud's last days that prefaces the Capataz's decision to grow rich is crucial to any understanding of the enigmatic conclusion to the novel. Decoud, alone on the Great Isabel, "after three days of waiting for the sight of some human face . . . caught himself entertaining a doubt of his own individuality" (p. 497). Sustained only by his love for Antonia Avellanos, having faith only in "the truth of his own sensations" (p. 229), he "was not fit to grapple with himself singlehanded." "Solitude from mere outward condition of existence becomes very swiftly a state of soul in which the affectations of irony and scepticism have no place. . . . In our activity alone do we find the sustaining illusion of an independent existence as against the whole scheme of things of which we form a helpless part. Decoud lost all belief in the reality of his action past and to come" (p. 497). Taking the ingots, he steers the lighter's dingy out into the gulf and commits suicide. "A victim of the disillusioned weariness which is the retribution meted out to intellectual audacity, the brilliant Don Martin Decoud, weighted by the bars of San Tomé silver, disappeared without a trace, swallowed up in the immense indifference of things" (p. 501).

Paradoxically, the pontifical censuring of skepticism is grounded in the pessimistic wisdom of cosmic irony. General irony disparages Decoud's less resourceful ironic temper. The entanglement of ironies prepares the way for the passage that immediately follows in which the same formulas are revised to describe Nostromo's situation. Decoud was not sufficiently dominated by love, by ideal sentiment, or by illusion. Nostromo, as much the servant of a violated illusion as he was of an ideal conception, is. The disappearance of the ingots, which he believes will be imputed to him, torments him. "And the spirits of good and evil that hover about a forbidden treasure understood well that the silver of San Tomé was provided now with a faithful and lifelong slave."

(pp. 501–2)
> *The magnificent Capataz de Cargadores, victim of the disenchanted vanity which is the reward of audacious action, sat in the weary pose of a hunted outcast through a night of sleeplessness as tormenting as any known to Decoud, his companion in the most desperate endeavor of his life. And he wondered how Decoud had died. But he knew the part he had played himself. First a woman*

> *[Teresa], then a man, abandoned both in their last extremity, for the sake of this accursed treasure. It was paid for by a soul lost and by a vanished life. The blank stillness of awe was succeeded by a gust of immense pride. There was no one in the world but Gian' Battista Fidanza, Capataz de Cargadores, the incorruptible and faithful Nostromo, to pay such a price.*

Both Nostromo and Decoud are victims of the immense indifference of things. But Nostromo's disenchantment seems simple and commonplace in comparison to Decoud's, which is a version of the punishment that may be meted out to an artist's skeptical distance from life.[13] The capacity for audacious action relies on Nostromo's primitive love of playacting: on his theatrical vanity and his superstitious nature. Ironically, in this as in all other respects, the Capataz is a morally minaturized example of true value. The capacity for illusion, which Decoud's disinterested truthtelling precludes, permits the only pride an ironic universe allows. The Capataz's fate involves the price and the reward of the futile and admirable achievement that Conrad sees in our struggle to countervail helplessness.

As foreman of the dream of statecraft, Nostromo served an illusion; enslaved to the violated treasure, he serves a lie. Much of Conrad's irony hovers about the distinction. In *Heart of Darkness*, Marlow proclaims that lies are detestable, tainted with death and flavored of mortality; Dr. Monygham finds lies odious. Yet there is no stable moral boundary between lies and illusions, delusions and ideal fictions. Once traditional fixed standards and true faiths give way, judgment and discrimination become equivocal. Were this not the case, Jim's story would lack the pathos of its point. Because Emilia's ideal conception is more worthy but no less illusory than Dr. Monygham's devotion or Gian' Battista's superstition, it invites irony. All ends, all men's goals, are flattened to the same futile level by cosmic indifference. Means, not ends, become the substance of our stories. Excepting the purblind tyrants and timeservers, all the characters in *Nostromo* are condemned to the pathetic and ironic task of dreaming goals out of mere means. Charles Gould's adulterous devotion to the mine, Cardinal-Archbishop Corbelán's plotting for the church; the revolutionism of the photographer who perches beside Nostromo's deathbed: each, no matter how vagrant, is accorded a touch of pathos; each error is an installment of the price exacted by a life in which all purposes are illusions.

The simplest, most vulgar of dreams is that of self-sufficiency and satisfaction. Nostromo is only a serviceable nature, but he is betrayed into the necessity of making his agency the firm ground of his identity. Like Willems in *An Outcast of the Islands*, he listens to the "whisper of deadly happiness, so sincere, so spontaneous, coming so straight from the heart—like every corruption. It was the voice of madness, of a delirious peace, of happiness that is infamous, cowardly, and so exquisite that the debased mind refuses to contemplate its termination" (pp. 141–42). Nostromo, better than Willems, knows that the material and sensual fulfillment he seeks violates some kind of taboo. Since his value, like all others, is debased, his service to himself is slavery to a corrupted treasure. His demoralization enacts the crass falling-off that forms the subject of the conversations between Dr. Monygham and Emilia near the end of the novel. She asks, "Will there be never any peace? Will there be no rest?"

(pp. 511–12)
> "No!" interrupted the doctor. "There is no peace and no rest in the development of material interests. They have their law and their justice. But it is founded on expediency, and is inhuman; it is without rectitude, without the continuity and the force that can be found only in a moral principle. Mrs. Gould, the time approaches when all that the Gould Concession stands for shall weigh as heavily upon the people as the barbarism, cruelty, and misrule of a few years back." . . .
> "Is it this we have worked for, then?"
> The doctor lowered his head. He could follow her subtle thought. Was it for this that her life had been robbed of all the intimate felicities of daily affection?

Monygham blames Charles Gould, and is too indignant with the "King of Sulaco" to pursue his bitter appraisal. Instead, he turns to Nostromo, who seems to contradict his dark prediction. "Ah! that fellow has some continuity and force. Nothing will put an end to him. But never mind that. There's something inexplicable going on—or perhaps only too easy to explain" (p. 512).

The details of the Capataz's mysterious behavior will be easily explained; the relation between this behavior and the competing ironies of the novel's ending is less straightforward. The doctor has heard rumors of a liaison between Gian' Battista and the Viola's younger daughter, Giselle. After Teresa's death, Giorgio and the two young women had been appointed, at Nostromo's request, keepers of the lighthouse just built on Great Isabel. The symbolic beacon, both practically valuable and morally misleading, intimates the condition of the state, the treasure, and the Capataz. Gian' Battista, now Captain Fidanza, is the sole visitor, coming and going on his trips to sell off small lots of the hidden silver. As he vowed, he is growing rich slowly. The elder daughter, Linda, like her mother dark, passionate, and sternly principled, adores Nostromo. She, her father, and Nostromo himself have long taken their engagement as settled. But now Linda's incorruptible character—a reminder of the original meaning invested in the service of the material treasure—abashes and repels the Capataz. He becomes infatuated with the sensual Giselle, a pretty, airy creature devoted to simple joys. Unlike Marlow in *Heart of Darkness*, Gian' Battista turns his back on the high principles of service to go ashore for a howl and a dance.

The great canvas of the novel appears to shrink to what Guerard terms a "simple romantic narrative," a popularized domestic drama that reflects the author's "temporary exhaustion."[14] Schwartz considers these "last chapters with their arabesque plot [to be] written more as romance than as mimetic novel."[15] But here as throughout Conrad's major fiction the conventions of romantic plotting represent a diminishment of the moral scope that gives life value and meaning; the absence of imaginative substance signals the cramped and specious private matter that must do duty for brave dreams. Nostromo's faithlessness echoes the "moral degradation of the idea" (p. 521) involved in Charles Gould's infidelity to Emilia and her dream. The slightly vulgar story of private cross-purposes and sorry mischances bears the full weight of the ironic reduction of high devotion to a commonplace existence. Desiring Giselle, Nostromo sets out to ask Giorgio for her hand. But the old man misunderstands; accustomed to think of Linda as Gian' Battista's intended, he sends for her instead of for her sister. Nostromo "was not afraid of being refused the girl he loved . . . but the shining spectre of the treasure rose before him, claiming his allegiance in a silence that could not be gainsaid. He was afraid, because, neither dead nor alive, like the Gringos on Azuera, he belonged body and soul to the unlawfulness of his audacity. He was afraid of being forbidden the island. He was afraid, and said nothing" (p. 531). Deprived of external validation, Nostromo now pursues a hole-and-corner life quite destitute of the glorious identity awarded his ideal service. A victim of hollowness without and within, he has no longer the wherewithal to feed his vanity with meaningful action. "To do things by stealth humiliated him. . . . A transgression, a crime, entering a man's existence, eats it up like a malignant growth, consumes it like a fever. Nostromo had lost his peace; the genuineness of all his qualities was destroyed. . . . His courage, his magnificence, his leisure, his work, everything was as before, only everything was a sham. But the treasure was real" (pp. 523–24).

Like Winnie Verloc, Gian' Battista is betrayed onto the threshold of the self-generated character that modern irony appears to demand. Like Winnie, he is quite unfit for the task of self-creation. The intensity of attention to the Capataz's reactions—a quasi-psychological focus absent from earlier comments—reveals only shame, hollowness, and the pain of lost truth. Insofar as Conrad continues the naturalists' concern with helpless people as protagonists of exceptional fates, illusion becomes for Nostromo, for Winnie, and more complexly, for Razumov the only possible ground for viable character. Without the protective shelter of a belief—and all beliefs are illusory—the treasure that decent figures contain is squandered. Yet treasure, itself an illusion, cannot be kept inviolate. Its betrayal is the ironic premise of human affairs. Not simply average natures, but a Charles Gould, a Decoud, a Dr. Monygham, and even an Emilia are stricken by the violation of their value-creating, validating faiths. Charles, for example, receives scant sympathy. But the parallel between his betrayal and Gian' Battista's, the abrupt shift of Dr. Monygham's discourse from the "king" to the now "miscalled Capataz de Cargadores" (p. 527), insinuates a general feeling of the pathos in the wake of disenchantment. Gian' Battista comes to resemble the faithless pilgrims of the Eldorado Exploring Expedition whom Marlow despises in *Heart of Darkness*. Yet the clichéd domestic drama and human insufficiency that mark Nostromo's decline are sadly antic rather than blameworthy. Moreover, beyond the speciousness of Captain Fidanza's new life—as beyond that of the Occidental Republic itself—something of the real value of his existence lingers on.

The joint devotion to the violated treasure and the captivating girl is an ironic parody of the theatrical service to the state and the courting of Pasquita at the beginning of the novel. In the manner of such parody, the inversion keeps alive through sardonic imitation the truth that is being betrayed. The vanity of self-abasement, a dim analogy to Dr. Monygham's story, recalls a less private vanity of devotion. Present pathos and past glory intermingle much in the fashion of Conrad's characteristic chiaroscuro of moral light and darkness. Gian' Battista shams an engagement to Linda while pursuing his love for her younger sister. He visits Giselle on the sly when his trips to carry off more ingots permit. She begs to be carried off as well, but he is not yet rich enough and tries to calm her by promising a "treasure of silver to buy a gold crown for thy brow."

(pp. 540–41)
> "A treasure?" she repeated in a faint voice, as if from the depths of a dream. "What is it you say?"
>
> She disengaged herself gently. He got up and looked down at her, aware of her face, of her hair, her lips, the dimples on her cheeks—seeing the fascination of her person in the night of the gulf as if in the blaze of noonday. . . .
>
> "A treasure of silver!" she stammered out. Then pressed on faster: "What? Where? How did you get it, Giovanni?"
>
> He wrestled with the spell of captivity. It was as if striking a heroic blow that he burst out—
>
> "Like a thief!"
>
> The densest blackness of the Placid Gulf seemed to fall upon

> his head. He could not see her now. She had vanished into a long, obscure abysmal silence, whence her voice came back to him after a time with a faint glimmer, which was her face.
> "I love you! I love you!"
> These words gave him an unwonted sense of freedom; they cast a spell stronger than the accursed spell of the treasure; they changed his weary subjection to that dead thing into an exulting conviction of his power.

Continuing the parallels and overlappings that weave his story into the center of the novel's design, Nostromo's reaching out for a sentimental dream to shelter him against the loss of the public power that had given his life meaning evokes the image of Decoud's reaching toward the beloved image of Antonia just before his desolate death. As Gian' Battista departs on yet another trip, Giselle's "form drooped consolingly over the low casement towards the slave of the unlawful treasure. The light in the room went out, and weighted with silver, the magnificent Capataz clasped her round her white neck in the darkness of the gulf as a drowning man clutches at a straw" (pp. 544-45).

Conrad has little patience with the belief that amatory relations can form an enclave of truth in a false or hollow world. As Decoud seeks a love stronger than his skepticism's truth, so Nostromo seeks in stolen silver and undemanding happiness for the protection of a stronger spell. The fiction is as facile as the private man, but the need is similar to that underlying Dr. Monygham's devotion to Emilia. The need impels the Capataz to Giselle's window on a night when she has warned him not to come. Hearing voices, Giorgio thinks that his daughter is with Ramirez, an amorous cargadore on whom she once cast a fond eye and whom the Garabaldino has forbidden the island. "I have shot Ramirez," the old man announces. "Like a thief he came, and like a thief he fell. The child had to be protected" (p. 554). Critically wounded, "the resourceful Capataz de Cargadores, master and slave of the San Tomé treasure," murmurs: "It seemed as though I could not live through the night without seeing thee once more—my star, my little flower" (p. 554). The theatrical prestige of inimitable action shrinks to the commonplace bathos of a thieving lover; the sustaining illusion of value, which had borne Nostromo's mark, leaves in the wake of its betrayal a man who cannot live alone through a single night.

The price Nostromo pays confirms Dr. Monygham's bleakest pessimism. Betrayed by those who have dreamed his value and by his own helpless simplicity, the Capataz occupies the general degeneration, half-courted and half-fated, that for Conrad increasingly shrouds the art of moral culture and the enterprise of civil protection. Yet neither Gian' Battista's genius nor the hope it serves is presented as unequivocally bankrupt. As Nostromo lies dying in the hospital, the narrative focus begins to return from private insufficiency to public meaning. Nostromo asks to speak to Emilia Gould. He tells her not to blame Giselle or Ramirez. The light-minded girl will soon forget and be forgotten. As for the man: "'No! It is not Ramirez who overcame the Capataz of the Sulaco Cargadores. . . . I die betrayed—betrayed by——' But he did not say by whom or by what he was dying betrayed" (p. 559). He cannot say. For the betrayal issues from the failure of deed to collaborate with word, material interests with ideal goals, the indifference of things with the dreams of men. Gian' Battista cannot speak to such vast matters. But he can at least clear his own good name by revealing the mystery of the lost ingots and Decoud's disappearance. Belief in his essential integrity and a populist rage at its futile exploitation frame his message.

(pp. 559–60; Conrad's ellipsis)

> "The silver has killed me. It has held me. It holds me yet. Nobody knows where it is. But you are the wife of Don Carlos, who put it into my hands and said, 'Save it on your life.' And when I returned, and you all thought it was lost, what do I hear? 'It was nothing of importance. Let it go. Up, Nostromo, the faithful, and ride away to save us for dear life!'"
>
> "Nostromo!" Mrs. Gould whispered, bending very low. "I, too, have hated the idea of that silver from the bottom of my heart."
>
> "Marvelous!—that one of you should hate the wealth that you know so well how to take from the hands of the poor. The world rests upon the poor, as old Giorgio says. You have always been good to the poor. But there is something accursed in wealth.

> *Señora, shall I tell you where the treasure is? To you alone. . . . Shining! Incorruptible!"*
>
> *A pained, involuntary reluctance lingered in his tone, in his eyes, plain to the woman with the genius of sympathetic intuition. She averted her glance from the miserable subjection of the dying man, appalled, wishing to hear no more of the silver.*
>
> *"No, Capataz," she said. "No one misses it now. Let it be lost forever."*

Outside Nostromo's room, Emilia meets Dr. Monygham who is "almost brutally" impatient to learn what the Capataz has told her. She lies: "He told me nothing." The doctor, though cherishing her as the one light in a dark world, does not believe her. "But her word was law. He accepted her denial like an inexplicable fatality affirming the victory of Nostromo's genius over his own. . . . he had been defeated by the magnificent Capataz de Cargadores, the man who had lived his own life on the assumption of unbroken fidelity, rectitude, and courage!" (p. 561).

The lie silences Monygham's skepticism. Gian' Battista is dying; the mystery of the treasure remains unsolved. Emilia sees herself as "surviving alone the degradation of her young ideal of life, of love, of work—all alone in the Treasure House of the World" (p. 522). The picture of utter loss suggests a meaning akin to the doctor's "cynical bitterness." Yet in these pages the assumption—the illusion—that the Capataz, the silver, and Emilia have served slips free from the fact of failure and degradation. Despite the class hatred in his words and despite the presence of the revolutionist photographer who hovers above the bed like the vulture above his ironic rebirth on Azuera, the tutelary spirit, essence, or gift contained in Nostromo's genius parts company with his thief's fate. The adjectives—"Shining! Incorruptible!"—that Nostromo applies to Mrs. Gould refer also to the ideal treasure and to the ideal resource he embodies. All meaning has been reduced to a moral condition as equivocal as Emilia's falsehood. But the denial of fact preserves as well as perverts. Told on behalf of communal order and protection, it affirms a continuing dedication. Just as Dr. Monygham's devotion allowed him to entertain an odious falsehood for

Emilia's sake, so Emilia's dream allows her to violate degraded fact on behalf of a bare fiction.

The lie, the treasure, Dr. Monygham's skepticism and devotion, the dream and its degradation, and the "inexplicable fatality" of Nostromo's genius are interwoven into the ambiguous irony of the novel's concluding lines. Giorgio has died of a stroke, leaving the sternly faithful Linda alone to tend the lighthouse. Dr. Monygham, who has rowed out to the island, shouts up to her the news of Nostromo's death.

> *"It is I who loved you," she whispered, with a face as set and white as marble in the moonlight. "I! Only I! [Giselle] will forget thee, killed miserably for her pretty face. I cannot understand. I cannot understand. But I shall never forget thee. Never!"*
>
> *She stood silent and still, collecting her strength to throw all her fidelity, her pain, bewilderment, and despair into one great cry.*
>
> *"Never! Gian' Battista!"*
>
> (p. 566) *Dr. Monygham . . . heard the name pass over his head. It was another of Nostromo's triumphs, the greatest, the most enviable, the most sinister of all. In that true cry of undying passion that seemed to ring aloud from Punta Mala to Azuera and away to the bright line of the horizon, overhung by a big white cloud shining like a mass of solid silver, the genius of the magnificent Capataz de Cargadores dominated the dark gulf containing his conquests of treasure and love.*

Lost on earth, the silver with its attendant dreams, falsities, and evil charms looms suspended above the scene. Dead, the Capataz enters the legendary field of the gringo treasure hunters who, "spectral and alive, are believed to be dwelling to this day . . . under the fatal spell of their success" (p. 5). In themselves, the factual gringos, if indeed they ever existed, were no doubt hollow men. Gian' Battista is scarcely more substantial. Decoud calls him "an exceptionally intelligent scoundrel" who, "like me, has come casually here to be drawn into the events for which his scepticism as well as mine seems to entertain a sort of passive contempt. . . . He does not seem to make any difference between speaking and thinking. Is it sheer naiveness or the practical point of view, I wonder?

Exceptional individualities always interest me, because they are true to the general formula expressing the moral state of mankind" (p. 246). Ironically, of course, the Capataz is exceptional in the naive perfection of his ordinariness; his intelligence is directed to the main chance. Asking only "to be well spoken of" (p. 246), he is a pure means available to any end. He inspires the sensual and materialistic passion of Pasquita and Giselle; he elicits Linda's transcendent fidelity. His admirers and detractors, lovers and exploiters, practice on him much as the many rhetoricians in the novel manipulate words. He is as serviceable as language itself: a kind of quixotic windmill that can function only when perceived to be something other than its simple self. Such availability is exceptional, enviable, and sinister. As long as the Goulds, the missionary capitalist Holroyd, and their supporters can sustain their effective vision of a spiritualized Realpolitik, Gian' Battista will sustain his service as Nostromo. When the vision fragments into separate, divisive dreams, the service too breaks down. Captain Fidanza pursues the vulgar prestige of self-aggrandizing romance.

Linda's fidelity, along with Captain Mitchell's enthusiasm, Decoud's curiosity and Dr. Monygham's irritated respect, mirror Conrad's intricate conception. Gian' Battista contains the potential for efficient action that should be educated to serve a traditional moral ethos. At the same time, the Capataz exists beyond the pale of moral education; he is a simple fatality, a pretext for illusion. Mysteriously, the man is an absence and a truth. His position attracts derisive skepticism and hopeful idealism. He is nothing and everything. In a way, his reality resembles the artifice that much late-century and early modern art would create out of prosaic and hollow fact. Taking Nostromo as its title, the novel pits an ambivalent version of this fiction against the force of general atrocity. Conrad's irony accepts the challenge of mediating between "things [that] seem to be worth nothing by what they are in themselves" and the "spiritual value" (p. 318) that may perhaps be refined from mereness. As in Cervantes's model for the interplay of worldly and spiritual ironies, so in Conrad's revision: illusion begets an ambiguously "true" reality. Cervantes's feeble Alonso Quijada or Quesada, the flat fellow whose very name is in doubt, becomes Don Quixote.

Gian' Battista becomes Nostromo. The created cognomen is like the state born out of the Goulds' vision. The primal "paradise of snakes" (p. 105) becomes the San Tomé mine "ablaze like a lighted palace above the dark Campo" (p. 485). The Campo peons, the lumpenproletariat once brutalized by the barbarous Guzman Bento, are transformed into workers on their way to civilization. Imagined into being by the dream, the state and its foreman are dependents of the dream. Because both are recalcitrant materials, both are exceptionally vulnerable to corroding skepticism and the disenchanting indifference that would cast them back into their rudimentary natures. Cervantes protects his knight through parodistic farce and ironic high comedy; Conrad envelops the dream and its servant, the material treasure and its creature, in an essentially defensive interplay of ironies.

Rising over Dr. Monygham's abased skepticism and Linda's cry into a cloudscape of irony, Nostromo's genius recalls the novel's epigraph: "So foul a sky clears not without a storm." The possibility of clearing persists despite the defeat of the stark truthtelling that the narrative shares with the doctor and Decoud and despite the defeat of the faith that the narrative idealizes in Emilia and Linda. Neither pessimism nor any traditional idealism can prevail. Since the novel is as skeptical of skepticism as it is of idealism, there is more of lingering light than critics have generally allowed. The Occidental Republic and the genius that helped bring it into being deserve neither Dr. Monygham's belittlement nor Linda's faith. The triumph of Nostromo's gifts is, and is not, illusory. The mere facts and their imaginative moral transformation invite a narrative mode similar to romantic irony: a fiction's apprehensions about the epistemological and ethical status of its own fictionality. Out of the entangling points of view, the mockery and the hope, arises a radically diminished but still functional moral value. In *The Secret Agent* and *Under Western Eyes*, even so hedged a remnant of Emilia's "ideal conception" will suffer reduction. In *Nostromo*, however, the Capataz's service still glimmers with the fictive yet true treasure mined by Emilia's dream.

III

THE SECRET AGENT
The Irony of Home Truths

THE IRONY THAT BLANKETS THE LONDON OF *The Secret Agent* seems far removed from the ambiguous interplay of sheltering illusion and innate disorder in *Lord Jim* and *Nostromo*. "Regulated hatred," the quality that D. W. Harding bestows on an aspect of Jane Austen's fiction in his controversial essay, aptly describes Conrad's narrative.[1] Almost every setting, character, and action mocks and is mocked by elusive moral judgments. Language itself is out of joint: adjectives become nouns, breaking faith with their function; negatives and negative prefixes abound, casting doubt on the simplest declaration; superlatives occur so often and so ludicrously as to travesty praise and blame. The novel is rich in those parallels, analogies, and cross-references through which Conrad elsewhere expresses the ambiguities of moral understanding. But by the end, when the Professor refuses to look at the "odious" masses that refuse to look at him, we find ourselves baffled. We remember Winnie's refusal to look deep into things; Sir Ethelred's refusal to listen to complications; the inability to see human meaning that stigmatizes Mr. Verloc and Comrade Ossipon. We seem near to grasping a pattern, but the overlappings yield only the opaqueness of coincidence. And yet the novel, for all its instances of absurdity and grossness, does not appear to most readers as an unsafe, threatening, or absurd experience. If the irony cruelly represents the deformity of value, it also works as in the previous novels to salvage a saving remnant of civilizing illusion.

Conrad's irony here has much in common with the idea of work that Marlow advocates in *Heart of Darkness*. The frequent foulness of London approximates in a sleezy, secondhand way the horrors of the Congo. Our plausible response would be to join those who avert their gaze. The irony, by holding offensiveness at bay, appears to allow us the safety of what Guerard calls an "entertainment."[2] The heavily melodramatic turns of plot are too excessive to touch us. As Schwartz puts it: "The reader shares the moral superiority, detachment, and condescension of the narrator. Conrad expects us to juxtapose the narrator's ironic redefinition of such terms as 'freedom' and 'knowledge' with definitions established by social and moral tradition."[3] The discrepancy between the spectacle of disorder and the reflexes of our moral beliefs frees us to be entertained. Just as Marlow's fidelity to his demanding work holds him safe from the Congo life all around him, so Conrad's irony seems at first to provide the support needed to endure an immersion in what Claire Rosenfield calls "this monstrous presence of stone and brick and darkness," this archetypal "world totally devoid of meaning."[4]

But the foulness is more insidious, immediate, and intimate than the distant heart of darkness. Repeatedly, the scenes and images press beyond the protection irony can offer. During the Assistant Commissioner's investigation of the Greenwich explosion in which Stevie is blown apart, he enters an Italian restaurant: "one of those traps for the hungry . . . without air, but with an atmosphere of their own" (p. 148). The irony summons up the response of stable understanding: we know that real meals and restaurants never live up to ideal expectation. Yet the next comment shocks us with its bitterness. The atmosphere is that of "fraudulent cookery mocking an abject mankind in the most pressing of its miserable necessities." Pushing beyond normative social satire, the narrative opens up a bleak perspective of human distress. Guerard sees in these lines a serious intrusion "of a different authorial consciousness and voice" from those which control the irony of the rest of the book.[5] Yet the view of the London wasteland is consistent. "Fraudulent," "abject," and "miserable" refer to the ugliness that the narrative presents as inevitably consequent on man's material necessities. The adjectives might be more appropriate to a traditional gnostic fury at the violation of spiritual integrity by the vile facts of our physical condition. Conrad, of course, is no Manichean. But the bloated flesh, ungainly needs, and offensive settings that engross *The Secret Agent* offer glimpses of a cosmic defamation quite as cruel as that which Hardy and other contemporary pessimists discover in the nakedness of the human situation.

The Secret Agent takes place in a grimly actualized version of those "mean streets" that Arthur Morrison and other observers of the London poor had been sentimentalizing. Both setting and cast correspond to the lower depths in which naturalistic fiction so often finds its case histories. However, unlike Zola's Paris, which is besotted by its lust for money, drink, or sex, Conrad's London is offensive in its very essence. The Verlocs' "domestic drama" (p. 222) illustrates a distasteful meanness that apparently expresses the city's truth. After Winnie learns of her husband's role in Stevie's death, she burrows into outraged silence. Enraged in his turn at her refusal to heed his own egocentric distress, Mr. Verloc accuses her of having shoved Stevie into his affairs and thus of being herself responsible for the young man's fate. "In sincerity of feeling and openness of statement, these words went far beyond anything that had ever been said in this home, kept up on the wages of a secret industry eked out by the sale of more or less secret wares: the poor expedients devised by a mediocre mankind for preserving an imperfect society from the dangers of moral and physical corruption, both secret, too, of their kind" (p. 258). The authorial distaste is aesthetic as well as moral. The dismal, fraudulent household is typical of the unsightly disease that afflicts most of the novel's milieus. In the manner of ironic discourse, the Verlocs' home perverts the meaning of home; the vehicle traduces the tenor. In *The Secret Agent*, moreover, as Schwartz observes, the "vehicles of a metaphor do not simply express a quality to be associated with the tenor, but replace the tenor as the essential quality of the imagined world."[6] Eclipsing instead of insinuating the truths they violate, the vehicles seem to cohere into a hermetically black vision of the way things are in London.

Yet London should be the home of the values to which Conrad's faithful seamen swear allegiance. By so grotesquely perverting these values, the city draws down some of the novel's most bitter irony. In much of his previous fiction, Conrad juggles two views of the homeland of moral service and order. Present-day

Britian is both a realm of flabby and complacent lives and a source of the civilizing force that supports moral endeavor. Traveling down the Congo, Marlow fondly recalls the trimmed lawns, hygienically packaged meats, and protective policemen in far-off London. If the city is overwrapped in comforts, it is nonetheless a safe shelter in a dark world. In *Lord Jim*, Marlow evokes with wry yet almost filial irony the comforts that protect those at home from the rending realities that cause Jewel to waste her life in tears. Home is peopled by women like Kurtz's Intended, who are too good and too vulnerable to bear stark truth, and by men like Jim's clergyman father, whose useful existence is supported by ignorance and by the bulwark of cultural platitudes. Distance blurs the tension between protection and evasion into Conrad's characteristic misty ambiguity. We are not unduly perplexed to realize that Jim is condemned for betraying the code of trust that cushions the lives of the tourists Marlow so disdains. But *The Scret Agent* tells a London story. Existence in the heartland of home appears to confirm all the negative judgments that have been diffused by distance and nostalgia. Not only is the earthbound city "emblematic of the complexity which Conrad sees as the particular characteristic of . . . shore moralities";[7] it is in itself a worse betrayer of faith than a Kurtz. Where from afar one saw a flickering beacon of moral truth, now one is mired in miserable corruption. As if Conrad were a Gulliver forced to confront in Brobdingnagian closeup the ideals on which the moral action of his previous fiction rests, the warts and more damaging disfigurations of home truths prove appalling.

Conrad's sense that this irony of disenchantment may seem excessive accounts for the defensive tone at the conclusion to his 1920 Author's Note. "But still I will submit that telling Winnie Verloc's story to its anarchistic end of utter desolation, madness and despair, and telling it as I have told it here, I have not intended to commit a gratuitous outrage on the feelings of mankind" (p. xv). Certainly Conrad's intense attention to what he calls the requirements of his art belies any suggestion of the gratuitous. Yet when decent, civilized citizens such as Winnie and her mother take over from dim African natives or Arab pilgrims as innocent victims, we do feel ourselves in the presence of outrageous melodrama. Nostromo's fate, of course, arouses a similarly painful sensation. But the Capataz's vanity and materialism in part blunt identification; moreover, even in his default and death the hope invested in his "genius" continues to resound. Nostromo is in his way an exceptional man. The "mediocre mankind" of *The Secret Agent* is, in Guerard's words, "flabby, debased, eternally gullible."[8] The best that Winnie and her kin can aspire to is that heroism of the commonplace often cherished by English moral realism of the previous century. And even such aspiration is unpleasantly disallowed. When Winnie's mother gets herself admitted to the home for worthy widows so that Mr. Verloc will be burdened only by poor Stevie, the cab that takes her to her exile mocks her good intentions. "The conveyance awaiting them would have illustrated the proverb that 'truth can be more cruel than caricature,' if such a proverb existed. Crawling behind an infirm horse, a metropolitan hackney carriage drew up on wobbly wheels and with a maimed driver on the box. This last peculiarity caused some embarrassment. Catching sight of a hooked iron contrivance protruding from the left sleeve of the man's coat, Mrs. Verloc's mother lost suddenly the heroic courage of these days" (pp. 155–56). The grotesque requires ironic distancing; but the irony carries the mother's admirable act into caricature.

In the Author's Note, Conrad speaks of his "vision of . . . a monstrous town more populous than some continents and in its man-made might as if indifferent to heaven's frowns and smiles; a cruel devourer of the world's light" (p. xii). London is now a blackness into which the moral clarity and civilizing purpose associated with light disappear. Conrad's pessimism, his sense of cosmic indifference and human deficiency, is condensed into the city, which becomes the urban ground of general irony. Although the terrorist Professor, the self-styled "moral agent" (p. 80) of explosive anarchy, is shown to be as mediocre as the masses he loathes, the sick city lends plausibility to his scorn. Commenting on the words "madness and despair," used both in the Author's Note and in the newspaper report of Winnie's fate, he proclaims "doctorally": "There are no such things. All passion is lost now. The world is mediocre, limp, without force. And madness and despair are a force. And force is a crime in the eyes of the fools, the weak and the silly who rule the roost" (p. 309). Not only is conventional life in the

Professor's view "open to attack at every point" (p. 68); as the novel presents it, the city's life deserves to be attacked. The Professor wants to strike "a blow fit to open the first crack in the imposing front of the great edifice of legal conceptions sheltering the atrocious injustice of society" (p. 80). The black anarchist's shabby motives ridicule this plan of vengeance; and Conrad, of course, mocks the very idea of radical action. But the fact of outrageous injustice and the odious disjunction between things as they are and as they ought to be appear to demand nothing less than revolution.

Foolish trust, debilitating misery, and blind routine dominate the life of the monstrous town. Most of the characters cannot or will not see. Were they Conrad's readers, he would have to admit failure in his ambition: "by the power of the written word to make you hear, to make you feel . . . before all, to make you *see*."[9] Winnie and her mother are prototypical in their intuition that direct perception of the world around them would be catastrophic. The intuition is correct. The turning point for Winnie, the beginning of her end, comes when she is able to see, to visualize, Stevie's destruction. Only the Professor and Stevie, however blinkered by their myopias, perceive some of the truths that the others evade or pervert. The Professor's personality and ideas reduce rational scorn of the general decadence to absurdity. Though far more appealing, Stevie's "convulsive sympathy" does the same. His response to the cabman and his "steed of apocalyptic misery" (p. 167) demonstrates his ability to feel but carries his ideal sentiments into a realm more cruelly grotesque than caricature. "He could say nothing; for the tenderness to all pain and misery, the desire to make the horse happy and the cabman happy, had reached the point of a bizarre longing to take them to bed with him. And that, he knew, was impossible" (p. 167). Stevie is naked before the irony he embodies. He is vulnerable perception unaided by any possibility of acting on what he feels. His raging sense of frustration parallels the Professor's.

(p.169)
> *At the bottom of his pockets his incapable, weak hands were clinched hard into a pair of angry fists. In the face of anything which affected directly or indirectly his morbid dread of pain, Stevie ended by turning vicious. A magnanimous indignation swelled his frail chest to bursting, and caused his candid eyes to*

> squint. Supremely wise in knowing his own powerlessness, Stevie was not wise enough to restrain his passions. The tenderness of his universal charity had two phases as indissolubly joined and connected as the reverse and obverse sides of a medal. The anguish of immoderate compassion was succeeded by the pain of an innocent but pitiless rage.

Stevie is the obverse of the Professor, who is not wise enough to know his own powerlessness. Both are bombs manufactured by London's reality. At issue is the need for some power to make sense of this reality. Both Stevie's judgment and the countervailing force it cries out for are movingly direct: "Poor brute, poor people," "Shame!" "Bad world for poor people" (p. 171). The episode is harrowing yet also antic. Our reaction might well resemble that suggested a few pages earlier when the grotesquely miserable cabman explains that his travail supports a "missus and four kids at 'ome." "The monstrous nature of that declaration of paternity seemed to strike the world dumb" (pp. 166–67). The irony joins two premises: that as humane people we ought to be struck dumb; that as weak people seeking protection from facts we will take refuge in dismissive amusement. Such irony enacts the defensive function of black humor: the hyperbole screens us from the pain just as the persistent wordplay—"magnanimous . . . frail chest"; "candid . . . squint"—blunts too naked an involvement in the action. The strategy realizes the implications of Marlow's bafflement in *Lord Jim* when Jewel's irremediable plight drives all his words into a "chaos of dark thoughts." Marlow's own extensive verbal work strives to preserve "the sheltering conception of light and order which is our refuge" (p. 313) while acknowledging the cruel facts that make this refuge a sham or an illusion. His irony compromises both the pure light of civilization and the blackness of real horror. The irony of *The Secret Agent* condenses horror into hyperbole, moral light into what Cooper calls Winnie's "amoral nobility,"[10] and the necessity for unpalatable compromise into the verbal game that civilization must by its powerless nature play.

Stevie and the Professor stand ouside the game. Winnie is both the game and its stakes. Near the end, after she discovers the truth about her husband and kills him, she is cast adrift. She tries to communicate her pain, isolation, and dread to the squalid, thick-skulled Comrade Ossipon. He has no idea what she is trying to express; she, reduced to a state much like that Stevie experiences when confronted with the cab and its "perfection of grotesque misery" (p. 170), cannot find words. But whereas Stevie elicits a tragicomic irony, Winnie calls forth one of the few clearly reliable expressions of narrative sympathy: "She lamented aloud her love of life, that life without grace or charm, and almost without decency, but of an exalted faithfulness of purpose, even unto murder. And, as so often happens in the lament of poor humanity rich in suffering but indigent in words, the truth—the very cry of truth—was found in a worn and artificial shape picked up somewhere among the phrases of sham sentiment" (p. 298). The passage recalls Flaubert's celebrated gloss on the way the jaded roué Rodolphe dismisses Emma Bovary's clichéd cry of love: "Human speech is like a cracked kettle on which we tap crude rhythms for bears to dance to, while we long to make music that will melt the stars."[11] Flaubert strives to perfect an art that will transform crude reality into enduring music. The irony that Conrad undertakes follows from the premise that the only hope of music in a universal dissonance is bound into human crudeness. Average men and women with their uncharming natures and shopworn hopes are as disenchanting a subject for art as London is a depressing setting for culture. Both as artistic and as moral material, Winnie is so minimal as to be grotesque. That the task of ironic protection has been reduced to the mean measure of Winnie, Stevie, and her mother helps account for the sense of infuriation that underlies so much of the novel. Outrage vies with pathos, each with its own irony.

The competing impulses create frustrating ambiguity in the work of irony that parallels the devious efforts of the police when their work of social protection runs up against the incomprehensible Greenwich explosion. The bomb that splatters Stevie across the park satisfies in its way the goal that Mr. Vladimir sets for Mr. Verloc. The nasty First Secretary of the foreign embassy wants to arouse the nation by "an act of destructive ferocity so absurd as to be incomprehensible, inexplicable, almost unthinkable; in fact, mad" (p. 33). And indeed, Chief Inspector Heat, the very model of a complacent, conventional policeman, is aghast. "The complexion of that case had somehow forced upon him the general idea of the absurdity of things human, which in the abstract is sufficiently annoying to an unphilosophical temperament, and in concrete instances becomes exasperating beyond endurance" (p. 91). Exasperation undermines efficiency—in policework as in ironic art. Heat's vexed bewilderment awakens in his superior, the Assistant Commissioner of police, "a special kind of interest in his work of social protection . . . a sudden and alert mistrust of the weapon in his hand" (p. 103). In the passage already quoted in the Introduction, Heat, sensing that the case is about to be taken out of his hands, feels

(pp. 116–17) *like a tight-rope artist might feel if suddenly, in the middle of the performance, the manager of the Music Hall were to rush out of the proper managerial seclusion and begin to shake the rope. Indignation, the sense of moral insecurity engendered by such a treacherous proceeding joined to the immediate apprehension of a broken neck, would, in the colloquial phrase, put him in a state. And there would be also some scandalized concern for his art, too, since a man must identify himself with something more tangible than his own personality, and establish his pride somewhere, either in his social position, or in the quality of the work he is obliged to do.*

Not only is Heat undone by his perception of what Conrad calls absurdity and many modernists term entropy; the entire system of protection in which the Chief Inspector finds his worthwhile meaning is cast into doubt. Like Winnie, who is equally literal-minded and equally faithful of purpose, Heat cannot grasp the unlikely nature of his service. He understands crime as a misapplied idea of industry resulting from "imperfect education" (p. 92). "Thieving was not a sheer absurdity" (p. 91). But such a view cannot comprehend the destructive ferocity of the Professor, the preposterous behavior of the mock anarchists who surround Mr. Verloc, or the bizarre inefficiency of language. As only the Assistant Commissioner will be able to see—and he quite dimly—protection cannot function except through an ironic sense of reality's treacherous proceedings.

Winnie's life suggests why. If policework echoes the way irony must function, Winnie's small art encapsulates what irony must protect. In one of those usages that undermine and then reconstitute the meaning of words, the narrative refers several times to her "philosophy," which consists in "not taking notice of the inside of facts" (p. 154). Denying all distracting complications in life, she directs the entire "ardour of [her] protecting compassion" (p. 58) on her brother. Protecting Stevie's "difficult existence," she has achieved a "life of single purpose and of a noble unity of inspiration, like those rare lives that have left their mark on the thoughts and feelings of mankind" (p. 242). Abjuring her one true love, the butcher who has money enough to support her but not Stevie, she settles on Mr. Verloc and the protection she believes he will extend to her family. Her commonplace heroism and moral art as well as her unglamorous faithfulness place her in the same tradition of nineteenth-century moral realism that is subjected to irony when her mother enters the home for widows. But Winnie is a larger subject and the irony is more intense. The reference to rare lives is countered at once: "But the visions of Mrs. Verloc lacked nobility and magnificence" (p. 242). Superlative praise dangles on a tightrope above the demeaning picture of a charmlessness so complete as to suggest a grotesquerie of being itself. Winnie purchases "seven years' security for Stevie loyally paid for on her part" (p. 243) by a marital service that seems as miserable a necessity as mankind's need for food; during these years, security grows "into confidence, into domestic feeling, stagnant and deep like a placid pool" (p. 243). Seeing Mr. Verloc at last take an interest in Stevie, whom he wants to employ in the Greenwich outrage, she believes that her work has triumphed: "And this last vision had such plastic relief, such nearness of form, such a fidelity of suggestive detail, that it wrung from Mrs. Verloc an anguished and faint murmur, reproducing the supreme illusion of her life. . . . 'Might have been father and son' "(p. 244). Fostering Stevie's destruction, Mr. Verloc ravages Winnie's illusion and her art. Her temperament, "when stripped of its philosophic reserve, was maternal and violent"; she regards her fate "with the rage and dismay of a betrayed woman" (p. 241). In a novel in which only betrayal and degrading injustice—whether enforced by Mr. Vladimir on Mr. Verloc or society on the silly Michaelis—create sympathy, the betrayal of Winnie's trust is rending.

Pathos, however, does not diminish irony. Winnie's art and home rest on near-ridiculous materials: a retarded boy and a flyblown smut shop, "a perfection of grotesque misery and weirdness of macabre detail." The idea of this stagnant, superficial wife of a bungling double agent as any kind of artist is absurd. Yet the irony rescues value of a sort. The shelter Winnie would create is no mean illusion. Throughout the sections leading to the disastrous revelation and the murder of Mr. Verloc, the narrative insinuates the kind of sad admiration that we observed in Marlow's ironic respect for the chief accountant in *Heart of Darkness*.

Repeatedly, the ironic hyperbole sets Winnie's predicament against the background of the primal state out of which civil order has emerged. When Mr. Verloc first gives evidence of duplicity, unaccountably withdrawing the family savings and bringing the cash home, Winnie suddenly distrusts the safety she has worked for. "This abode of her married life appeared to her as lonely and unsafe as though it had been situated in the midst of a forest" (p. 201). Later, having finally understood that Stevie, the "presiding genius" of this abode, is dead, "Mrs. Verloc gazed at the whitewashed wall. A blank wall—perfectly blank. A blankness to run at and dash your head against. . . . She kept still as the population of half the globe would keep still in astonishment and despair, were the sun suddenly put out in the summer sky by the perfidy of a trusted providence" (p. 244). The total eclipse releases Winnie "from all earthly ties. She had her freedom" (p. 251). But freedom demands a force commensurate to a precivilized absolutism of events. Winnie, now that her small art is undone, is as powerless as Stevie. For her, freedom is a more annihilatingly heroic challenge than it will be for Razumov in Conrad's next novel. "Her intention had been simply to get outside the door for ever. And if this feeling was correct, its mental form took an unrefined shape corresponding to her origin and station. 'I would rather walk the streets all the days of my life,' she thought. But this creature, whose moral nature had been subject to a shock of which, in the physical order, the most violent earthquake of history could be only a faint and languid rendering, was at the mercy of mere trifles, of casual contacts" (p. 255).

The conceits magnify both Winnie's plight and her insufficiency. The rhetoric aspires to the naked embattlement of truths engendered by Kurtz's bestial horror, Jim's struggle for honor in primal Patusan, and Nostromo's fall from service into a vain grasping for his ego's survival. Winnie tumbles into the darkness that Marlow once saw as extending from savage Africa to the estuary of the Thames. She puts into the knife thrust that kills her husband "all the inheritance of her immemorial and obscure descent, the simple ferocity of the age of caverns, and the unbalanced nervous fury of the age of bar-rooms" (p. 263). But even as a primal actor Winnie is banal and shallow. "Mrs. Verloc, who always refrained from looking deep into things, was compelled to look into the very bottom of this thing. She saw there no haunting face, no reproachful shade, no vision of remorse, no sort of ideal conception. She saw there an object. That object was the gallows. Mrs. Verloc was afraid of the gallows" (p. 267).

The resonant amplification of Winnie's fate is cut short by an almost childlike syntactic simplicity. If many of the images cast her as an exceptional victim of the cruelty meted out to average humanity by a perfidious universe, the strong ironic current reminds us that the sister is but the other side of the brother's thin coin. Unlike Zola's Gervaise or Hardy's Tess, whose predicament is similarly extreme, Winnie is not so much average as she is flat. Her betrayal is plangently evoked, but she is a mere descendant of Mrs. Micawber and Mrs. Gradgrind. After the loss of Stevie—"the salt of passion in her tasteless life" (p. 174)—and the murder of her husband, she stands on the threshold of the multidimensionality that might grant individuality and meaningful freedom. But she cannot develop; she is quite without even Nostromo's vain flair. Her single passion, her "exalted faithfulness of purpose," ratifies flatness: Stevie is her Mr. Micawber.

With Winnie, Conrad presents a supreme instance of essential simplicity interwoven with a grandly ambiguous moral action. Her fixed idea torn away, Winnie becomes flotsam. Harrowed by her terror of the gallows, she is as stricken of refuge as the friendless, solitary orphan Razumov. "The vast world created for the glory of man was only a vast blank to Mrs. Verloc. She did not know which way to turn. Murderers had friends, relations, helpers—they had knowledge. She had nothing. She was the most lonely of murderers that ever struck a mortal blow. She was alone in London: and the whole town of marvels and mud, with its maze of streets and its mass of lights, was sunk in a hopeless night, rested at the bottom of a black abyss from which no unaided woman could hope to scramble out" (pp. 270–71). Instead of a source of light, London is the abyss of general irony, a moral quicksand dragging down all meaning. Blending outrageous comedy and ironic pathos, Ossipon's hope of exploiting Winnie's plight and her destitution, the long penultimate chapter exhibits the ravages of flatness. From the novel's first paragraph, in which Mr. Verloc leaves "his shop nominally in charge of his brother-in-law," Stevie, and his wife "in charge of his brother-in-law," (p. 3), the themes of interdependence and protection have been made to seem a mocking trap. Now Winnie is freed into an entrapping nothingness. Her smallness is even further reduced. Yet it is just in this context that she receives the homage already quoted: her life, charmless and "almost without decency," has been "of an exalted faithfulness of purpose, even unto murder."

Human minimalism and the truth of Conrad's idea are now inextricable. As Cooper writes, Winnie becomes " an heroic figure in the environment of London's squalor."[12] The narrative seems to practice a diminished version of Emilia Gould's "imaginative estimate" that finds in the raw silver—and by extension in its simple foreman—"a justificative conception." As in *Nostromo*, this conception resides ironically and painfully not in the glory of principled action but in the stolid limitations of charmless common needs. Winnie is the principle that civilization serves pressed flat. Her thinness protects her from the often luridly scornful irony directed at the miasma in which she is found while at the same time protecting the reader from too sheer an empathy with her "anarchistic end of utter desolation."

But even this precarious affirmation is subject to irony. As Winnie's qualities are a more serviceable form of her brother's simpleminded virtues, so Mr. Verloc's omnivorous yet inert egoism is the debased but logical image of Winnie's limitations. Central among the "figures grouped about Mrs. Verloc and related directly or indirectly to her tragic suspicion that 'life doesn't stand much looking into' " (pp. xii–xiii), Mr. Verloc reduces the irony of moral realism to the status of simple delusion. He is that antimatter implied by the kind of matter Winnie embodies. He translates her stubborn fidelity into almost archetypal inertia; his corrosive egoism is the vile implication of the moral torpor apparent in his wife, in her mother, and in the London masses. Attuned only to his own needs, Mr. Verloc is blind to all others. "Mr. Verloc lacked profundity. Under the mistaken impression that the value of individuals consists in what they are in themselves, he could not possibly comprehend the value of Stevie in the eyes of Mrs. Verloc" (p. 233). Stevie's value expresses that mixture of illusion, moral truth, and faith that allows us to be more than our unaided personalities. Mr. Verloc is the nemesis of such value. He exudes "the air common to men who live on the vices, the follies, or the baser fears of mankind; the air of moral nihilism common to keepers of gambling hells" (p. 13). He leeches out the meaning of human community. Gloating over the comfortable protection he observes in the wealthy district surrounding Mr. Vladimir's embassy, he

(p. 12)
> would have rubbed his hands with satisfaction had he not been constitutionally averse from every superfluous exertion. . . . He was in a manner devoted to [idleness] with a sort of inert fanaticism, or perhaps rather with a fanatical inertness. Born of industrious parents for a life of toil, he had embraced indolence from an impulse as profound, as inexplicable, and as imperious as the impulse which directs a man's preference for one particular woman in a given thousand. He was too lazy even for a mere demagogue. . . . It was too much trouble. He required a more perfect form of ease; or it might have been that he was the victim of a philosophical unbelief in the effectiveness of every human effort.

Mr. Verloc's force, like Satan's, is that of negation. He strains the order of syntax and baffles words. Not the Professor's terrorism, certainly not the shabby revolutionism of his colleagues, but the double agent's negation of all mankind's efforts at effective meaning—an incarnation of the Schopenhauerian Will that undoes human intentions—is the true anarchy. Since the irony of the novel parallels Conrad's ideal of valuable work, Mr. Verloc is the irony's archenemy.

The secret agent's parasitism recalls the way in which Lantier in Zola's *L'Assommoir* saps the industrious aspirations of the families he invades. But Lantier is spawned by what Zola sees as a decadent era, by a historical situation that may be superseded; Mr. Verloc emerges from the darkness that Conrad sees as separating the moral illusions that give life structure from an ever-present primal disorder. The treacherous husband not only adopts the protective coloration of valuable illusion; he embodies the terrifying cohabitation of the arts of meaninglessness with the works of faith. Marrying Winnie, he transforms the sanctuary of home into the nihilism of a disorderly house. The Assistant Commissioner can tell Sir Ethelred that Mr. Verloc has a "genuine wife and a genuinely, respectably, marital relation. . . . Yes, a genuine wife. And the victim was a genuine brother-in-law. From a certain point of view we are here in the presence of a domestic drama" (pp. 221–22). With Mr. Verloc, however, "genuine" and "domestic" are stripped of meaning—as are most other words of value in the narrative he so infects. The agent performs an act of vampirism on "the sheltering conception . . . which is our refuge." His insidious subversion of order places him in the company, not of the obviously evil Kurtz and Gentlemen Brown, but of James Wait and the faithless pilgrims of the Eldorado Exploring Expedition.

Since civilization relies upon the interdependent integrity of all its components, the threat Mr. Verloc incarnates is a matter of public as well as domestic drama. He undermines the protective structure that holds Mr. Vladimir and the Professor at bay. Carrying out the former's plan for a gratuitous blasphemy to be directed at learning—at the moral education central to Victorian culture—he plays into the hands of the alien ambitions that would overturn all Western civilization. The bomb that kills Stevie awakens the fear of foreign intentions common to the period: the kind of apprehension that underlies Erskine Childers's celebrated spy novel, *The Secret of the Sands* (1903). The suspicion that something more than "barefaced audacity amounting to childishness of a peculiar sort" (p. 138) may be involved in the affair brings first the Assistant Commissioner and then the Home Minister, Sir Ethelred, into the investigation. Both men fear that home in its largest meaning may be in jeopardy.

Public protection is, however, just as involved in irony as the shelter Winnie tries futilely to create for Stevie. The Assistant Commissioner seems at first a more efficient enforcer of the values of the home service than the credulous wife. Straddling the gap between London truths and the bright illusions of moral empire, keenly aware of the ironic ambiguities of the game civil order must play, the Assistant Commissioner appears to carry something of the glamour of Conradian high drama into the entropic settings appropriate to Mr. Verloc.[13] Not only does the Assistant Commissioner solve the mystery of the Greenwich outrage; he generates the sole instant resembling moral satisfaction that the novel allows: the expulsion of Mr. Vladimir from the civilized precincts of the Explorers Club, that "building of noble proportions and hospitable aspect" (p. 228). The gifts of this "born detective" (p. 117) have been developed by policework in the colonies, where issues are straightforward and possibilities for action still bright. The colonies nurture the clue to effective detection, which is also the key to the work of irony: mistrust. But the colonies have been left behind. The Assistant Commissioner's socially ambitious wife, unable to abide life abroad, badgers him into returning home. The town galls him; he resents "the necessity of taking so much on trust" (p. 114). Even worse, he himself is forced to become the subject of his own mistrust. On the one hand, the Greenwich "affair, which, in one way or another, disgusted Chief Inspector Heat, seemed to him a providentially given starting-point for a crusade" (p. 222) against foreign meddling. Yet on the other hand, the high cause conceals a selfish motive. His wife's wealthy and influential patron has taken up the defense of the idealistic anarchist Michaelis. Chief Inspector Heat suspects Michaelis and wants to arrest him. Should Heat have his way and the "ticket-of-leave apostle" be sent back to prison, the Assistant Commissioner believes that "the distinguished and good friend of his wife, and himself" would never forgive him.

> (pp. 112–13) The frankness of such a secretly outspoken thought could not go without some derisive self-criticism. No man engaged in a work he does not like can preserve many saving illusions about himself. The distaste, the absence of glamour, extend from the occupation to the personality. It is only when our appointed activities seem by a lucky accident to obey the particular earnestness of our temperament that we can taste the comfort of complete self-deception. The Assistant Commissioner did not like his work at home. The police work he had been engaged on in a distant part of the globe had the saving character of an irregular sort of warfare or at least the risk and excitement of an open-air sport. . . . Chained to a desk in the thick of four millions of men, he considered himself the victim of an ironic fate—the same, no doubt, which had brought about his marriage.

In his distaste for domestication, for hole-and-corner action, for a world swaddled in secrecies and galling compromises, the Assistant Commissioner reflects the tone of the novel as a whole. In Guerard's words, this "may well be the author in a succinct if unconscious self-portrait. Yet the Assistant Commissioner evokes none of the major emotional involvement . . . we feel in the portrait of Razumov."[14] The Assistant Commissioner unravels the case and gets rid of Mr. Vladimir. But the corrosive irony that London represents becalms the possibility of sympathy as it swallows the meaning of successful detection. However appealing this man with his "long, meagre face with the accentuated features of an energetic Don Quixote" (p. 115), he simply disappears from the final quarter of the novel, apparently carrying with him what few saving illusions the narrative offers.

Winnie can kill her husband; the Assistant Commissioner can solve the mystery. Neither can counteract the banal, anonymous horror for which Mr. Verloc stands. Winnie is freed and forced from home into the mean streets. Seeking succor, she puts her trust in the unsavory Ossipon, one of her husband's cabal. He robs and then deserts her, leaving her on the boat train while he strolls home. "And again Comrade Ossipon walked. His robust form was seen that night in distant parts of the enormous town slumbering monstrously on a carpet of mud under a veil of raw mist. It was seen crossing the streets without life and sound. . . . He walked through Squares, Places, Ovals, Commons, through monotonous streets with unknown names where the dust of humanity settles inert and hopeless out of the stream of life" (p. 300). The perpetrator of the last of the novel's betrayals blends into the ugly murk that has obscured Winnie and the Assistant Commissioner. Reaching his "small grimy house" with its "mangy grassplot" (p. 300), Ossipon ratifies the general inertia by falling asleep in the daylight.

Mr. Verloc's qualities seem to spread from his corpse over the town. His inheritance funds the brief final chapter that recounts a conversation between Ossipon and the Professor. The description of the latter's lodgings presses unpleasantness into odium. "The room was large, clean, respectable, and poor with that poverty suggesting the starvation of every human need except mere bread. There was nothing on the walls but the paper, an expanse of arsenical green, soiled with indelible smudges here and there, and with stains resembling faded maps of uninhabited continents" (p. 302). The initial adjectives recall the home that Winnie worked for; the poisonous poverty brings to mind Stevie's reaction to the cabman and his nag; the reference to the violence done to human need echoes the comment on the Italian restaurant. But just as the maplike stains suggest no known region, so the cross-references suggest no interpretation that can sustain analysis.

Both in itself and as a conclusion to the narrative, the scene balks any meaning other than its offensiveness. Yet we are aware that some stronger value must be nearby. The irony, for all its variousness, continually summons up a context of evaluation that we all share. Meanwhile, the Professor rants on, and his spite still seems a plausible reaction to the omnipresent bleakness. He would rid the world of "the weak, the flabby, the silly, the cowardly, the faint of heart, and the slavish of mind. They have power. They are the multitude. Theirs is the kingdom of the earth. Exterminate, exterminate! . . . First the blind, then the deaf and the dumb, then the halt and the lame—and so on. Every taint, every vice, every prejudice, every convention must meet its doom" (p. 303). We remember Kurtz's gloss on his report to the International Society for the Suppression of Savage Customs: "Exterminate all the brutes!" This new version, concocted of black anarchism and perverted Nietzscheanism, is equally outrageous. Imperialism must civilize; civilization must protect. But the Professor's wrath hardly understates the depravities that the city exhibits. Faith and fact, fiction and falsity, meaning and absurdity have been subject to so many doublings, overlappings, and contortions that one might well wish to wipe the slate clean and begin anew. Push the almost inert, stubborn decency of Winnie and her mother a fraction farther and we arrive at her husband's horror; press merited distaste to its conclusion and we join the Professor's loathing.

Indeed, the Professor is the bomb in the grip of the novel's irony. He is the barely human point at which horror and ugliness collapse into a moral standoff: into the perilous ambiguity that may conceal the mere possibility of something better. His capsule biography much earlier in the narrative predicts his function. His "considerable natural abilities" having been unrewarded by his teachers, his ambitions frustrated, his eyes were opened as a young man "to the true nature of the world, whose morality was artificial, corrupt, and blasphemous" (pp. 80–81). He became a rebel.

(p. 81)
> *The way of even the most justifiable revolutions is prepared by personal impulses disguised into creeds. The Professor's indignation found in itself a final cause that absolved him from the sin of turning to destruction as the agent of his ambition. . . . He was a moral agent—that was settled in his mind. By exercising his agency with ruthless defiance he procured for himself the appearances of power and personal prestige. That was undeniable to his vengeful bitterness. It pacified its unrest; and in their own way the most ardent of revolutionaries are perhaps doing no more but seeking for peace in common with the rest of mankind—the peace of soothed vanity, of satisfied appetites, or perhaps of appeased conscience.*

Although the Professor is the only ardent revolutionary in the novel, the passage diffuses his uniqueness. Sharing the insufficiency of flat mankind, he is in his frightful way fulfilling a common, miserable human need. The explosive and detonator that he always carries close to hand conform absurdly to the common rule: "a man must identify with something more tangible than his own personality." The Professor's goal reduces the formula to madness; but the maddened instance underscores the formula's truth.

Revolution here is a gross aberration of man's need to buttress selfhood in some larger meaning. The Professor's creed is in line with all other illusions. The terrorist is a fearsome horror. But his fearful loathing of other men expresses his awareness that he cannot escape the common denominator of human fact. His cringing and demeaning hatred is at the same time the irreducible remnant of Conrad's faith in civil order. The city's millions defame dreams and ideal conceptions; but they also defuse the nightmare the Professor promises. He "felt the mass of mankind mighty in its numbers. They swarmed numerous like locusts, industrious like ants, thoughtless like a natural force, pushing on blind and orderly and absorbed, impervious to sentiment, to logic, to terror, too, perhaps. This was the form of doubt he feared most. . . . What if nothing could move them? Such moments come to all men whose ambition aims at a direct grasp upon humanity—to artists, politicians, thinkers, reformers, or saints" (pp. 81–82). If as Guerard observes "the obsessed Professor pushes certain ideas of the author to a dangerous extreme,"[15] the mass of men embody the hope at the farthest reach of the author's irony.

Conrad has followed the mutation of moral exceptionalism into a bizarre shelter in a seeming dead end. Jim's imagination of self-creation based on popular tales is a first stage toward this end; Nostromo's unlikely potential for moral service goes even farther in the direction of diminished glory. The cast of *The Secret Agent* carries the reduction as far as it will go. In the last paragraph the Professor disappears, swallowed like Winnie and her kin, like Mr. Verloc, like the Assistant Commissioner, by the inert natural force that is the only antidote to the force of scorn. "And the incorruptible Professor walked, too, averting his eyes from the odious multitude of mankind. He had no future. He disdained it. He was a force. His thoughts caressed the images of ruin and destruction. He walked frail, insignificant, shabby, miserable—and terrible in the simplicity of his idea calling madness and despair to the regeneration of the world. Nobody looked at him. He passed on unsuspected and deadly, like a pest in the street full of men" (p. 311).

Again, Conrad's image becomes clearer if compared to Zola's treatment of a similar scene. The last glimpse of the Professor echoes the parting evocation of the black anarchist Souvarine in *Germinal*. After destroying the mine that sustains good workers and bad capitalists alike, Souvarine heads "yonder, somewhere into the unknown." "It would be he, no doubt, whom the expiring bourgeoisie would hear beneath them as the very paving stones exploded under their feet."[16] Zola, while portraying Souvarine as terrifying and abhorrent, stands behind the vision of decadence and injustice crying out for destruction. No individual, he believes, but a vengeful burgeoning of the masses will accomplish the inevitable regeneration. By contrast, the quality of Conrad's natural force has no clear meaning at all. Its value is an ironic parallel to Mr. Verloc's vampirism. Madness and despair, the key words flowing from Winnie's fate, are stifled in unsightly dust; the Professor is reduced to a pest. Like "the sound of exploding bombs," he will be lost in the "immensity of passive grains without an echo. For instance, this Verloc affair. Who thought of it now?" (p. 306). Zola sees the moral order that English moral realism associates with the best values of culture as a mystical attribute of the anonymous masses. The "people" will seed a germinal rebirth of value. Conrad's irony conveys only a flatness. The force, "blind and orderly and absorbed," that thwarts the Professor casts its pall as well on art and all other illusions of human aspiration. This almost entropic leveling of the protective virtue of culture gives weight to Stevie's judgment: "Bad world for poor people. Shame."

All value in *The Secret Agent* is grotesquely disadvantaged. It is true, as Schwartz argues, that the "*control* and *discipline* of [Conrad's] language, as opposed to the language of London, create an alternative to the world observed."[17] But the tone of the novel's ironic discourse conforms to the description of the Assistant Commissioner's work: "No man engaged in a work he does not like can preserve many saving illusions about himself. The distaste, the absence of glamour, extend from the occupation to the personality." In passage after passage, the language of irony has seemed to many readers an inhuman game with human needs. There are no saving illusions. The novel almost grudgingly permits the minimal illusion that protects a minimal achievement. But the self-consciousness that signals Conrad's version of romanic irony—his complex playing with the idea of civilization as fiction—now seems directed as much at the offensiveness of the fiction's raw materials as at the fictionality of true shelter. The strain of control, art, and irony is painfully apparent. Yet the flat faith and stolid order do finally hold meaninglessness and the horror of primal disorder at a remove. Language can still perform a protective work. We are not yet confronted with the utter cynicism that will betray all mankind's works in *Under Western Eyes*.

IV

UNDER WESTERN EYES
Irony and Women's Strength

FROM *HEART OF DARKNESS* TO *The Secret Agent* Conrad shapes stories into moral actions through irony. The irony expresses Conrad's endeavor to impose the artifact of moral culture upon the anarchistic facts of man's flaws and nature's indifference. As we have seen, however, this irony has its own dark side. It involves not only the creation of protective meaning in the face of recalcitrant realities but also a skepticism perilously close to that which dooms Decoud. Irony is an equivocal metaphoric mode in which the vehicle, instead of extending our understanding of the tenor, emphasizes the value of the tenor through antithesis, perversion, absence, or absurdity. The shortsightedness, egotism, or malignancy of human acts at times strikes the author's eyes as so abominable as to paralyze the devotion to human moral community that is the tenor his irony would convey. From Marlow's mockery of our complacencies to the sarcastic picture of home culture in *The Secret Agent* to Razumov's corrosive bitterness in *Under Western Eyes*, the resources of irony verge upon the reflexes of nihilism. There are many moments when one might rebuke Marlow or the narrative persona of *The Secret Agent* with the words that Sophia Antonovna addresses to Razumov when she instructs him to "leave off railing." Remember, she exclaims, "that women, children, and revolutionists hate irony, which is the negation of all saving instincts, of all faith, of all devotion, of all action" (p. 279). The blind or devoted faith of Kurtz's Intended, of the *Patna* pilgrims and Jewel, of the childish Nostromo and the visionary Antonia Avellanos, of Stevie and Winnie is the cherished burden undertaken by the masculine work of Conrad's irony. The special, and appalling, fact of *Under Western Eyes* is that heroic, manly irony collapses into futility and negation. The two potentialities of irony cancel each other. The assumptions of Conrad's moral action devolve into the tinsel shelter of the Genevan setting and the impotent judgments of the language teacher who serves as narrator. At the same time, the traditional Conradian division between women strong in faith but weak in their ability to forge protection and men who must act or speak on their behalf breaks down.

In its setting, its narrator, and its extended concern with the women who mirror or transform Razumov's plight, *Under Western Eyes* is the most feminine of Conrad's major novels. It is Conrad's most gruelingly psychological story, and psychology here arises out of the defeat of reason and practicality and the enforced dominance of instinct, feeling, and sensibility. Although the plot is grounded in political forces, Schwartz is surely right in stressing Conrad's "rejection of political commitment in favour of personal relationships and private commitments."[1] Razumov becomes the register of a total eclipse of meaning as devastating as that experienced by Kurtz or Decoud. But the sensation of sheer bereavement that Razumov undergoes has no extensive precedent among Conrad's men. The nakedness of this psyche bewitched by the nothingness of everything outside itself is closest to that dramatized in Jewel, Linda Viola, and Winnie. After Winnie stabs her husband, she falls to "the bottom of a black abyss from which no unaided woman could hope to scramble out" (p. 271). *Under Western Eyes* begins, unfolds, and concludes in this abyss. What Guerard, Frank Kermode, and others have interpreted as Conrad's ambivalent fascination with "*cosas de Russia*," is more nearly a horrified imaginative involvement in a realm that inverts Conrad's premises and hopes into something resembling antimatter.[2] The insistent supernatural nightmare imagery that Kermode views as a secret subtext of the novel is appropriate to an abyss that transmutes all previous values and virtues.

As has often been noted, the rape of Razumov's life that casts him into horror resembles Dostoevsky's most intense dramas. The parallel announces a pervasive irony both more direct and more immediately threatening to any hope of moral shelter than that Marlow encounters in primal Africa. For Dostoevsky is of course a byword in Conrad's lexicon for Russia's refusal of all that civilization should accomplish and represent. "I don't know what D. stands for or reveals, but I do know that he is too Russian for me. [*The Brothers Karamazov*] sounds to me like some fierce mouthings from prehistoric ages."[3] Razumov's hopes for a life of reason, practical service, and stability are blasted when the idealist assassin Haldin erupts into his room. Fate is an absurd crime, and Razumov's punishment is to fall into "Dostoevskyism."[4] Razumov is an intelligent, sensitive average man: "one of those men who, living in a period of mental and political unrest, keep an instinctive hold on normal, practical, everyday life. . . . his main concern was with his work, his studies, and with his own future" (p. 10). The Balzacian "one of those" casts the student as a type; he seems the kind of youth Marlow might welcome as a mate. There is little in the initial presentation to support the charge of egotistic amorality that Cooper and Schwartz expatiate upon.[5] From any normal or traditional point of view Razumov's self-concern and ambition are more a necessity of his situation than a fault. Deprived of family, a natural child who bears a label rather than a name (p. 14), he is "as lonely in the world as a man swimming in the deep sea" (p. 10). Any identity he can earn must be struggled for against great odds. His need and position are of course extreme, but hardly beyond the pale of the challenges that Victorian popular manuals of self-help associate with the worthy endeavor to achieve character. But this hard-pressed youth—and with him all traditional ideas of character, rationality, and decency—suffers the most outrageous betrayal in Conrad's extensive catalogue of betrayals.

Conrad's drama seems to play with the possibility that there is a meaning in Razumov's fate. Critics have seen the student as in some way responsible for his plight. Because he is blind to some true way or tenor, he becomes the self-created ironic vehicle of false values and choices. The absurdity heaped upon him is viewed as a Dostoevskian message rather than a prehistoric babble of events. For Dostoevsky, the human condition exists in absurd disjunction from Christ. Incoherence must be suffered if man is to transcend his ironic reality and obtain the fantastic truth of Christian salvation. All earthly structures—familial, social, and political—are fallen, perverted images of a divine idea. But not only does Conrad regard Dostoevsky's messianic fantastic irony as mumbo jumbo; he holds out no hope for any truth outside or beyond earthly action. Similarly, there seems to be a possible parallel between Razumov's violated life and that of Kafka's Joseph K. in *The Trial*, written only a few years after *Under Western Eyes*. The functionaries of the Law break in upon Joseph K. as abruptly as Haldin does upon Razumov. Like Haldin, the trial involves Kafka's protagonist in a network of issues and values beyond his self-enclosed interests. The novels share the premise of a violation that overturns normality and conventional responses. But the very word *Law*, however inscrutable and ironic in its purport, suggests an image, memory, or hope of meaning quite absent from Razumov's Russian drama. Moreover, while Joseph K.'s complacent self-satisfaction intensifies the possibility of a truth he cannot see, the rending finality of Razumov's sense of nakedness enforces an identification with the emptiness and meaninglessness of his situation. To be sure, other more modern writers than Conrad view versions of such nakedness as the permitting premise of what Gide terms freedom or what Rilke's Malte Laurids Brigge evokes as "the threshold of the voiceless silence of a real conflict."[6] Yet though it is possible to read Razumov's torture as a devastating prelude to unprecedented compassion, as a supreme example of the sacrifice demanded by man's need for sheltering moral culture, there is no equivalent in *Under Western Eyes* to any modern idea of freedom or self-creation. Such possibilities enter ambiguously into the stories of Kurtz and Lord Jim; Razumov's dreadful vacuum mocks the hope of selfhood let alone of freedom. "Everything abandoned him—hope, courage, belief in himself, trust in men. His heart had, as it were, suddenly emptied itself"(p. 303).

The immediate terms of the irony that seizes Razumov appear to be stable elements of a political fable. He is illegitimate and must seek his selfhood in the Russian commonweal. His "closest parentage was defined in the statement that he was a Russian. Whatever good he expected from life would be given to or withheld from his hopes by that connexion alone" (pp. 10–11). To keep alive his hope of connection, he betrays Haldin to his influential natural father who then helps him to bring his information to the proper authorities. In a kind of political reversal of the oedipal situation, his parentage murders his independent being; he becomes a marked man, a suspect, a puppet of autocracy. The political message seems clear. Russia is nihilism and inhumanity institutionalized. No good can come of it; no value can survive it. The West is wholly different: a humanly possible civilization. If a "man's real life is that accorded to him in the thoughts of other men by reason of respect or natural love" (p. 14), then Russia, denying any respect or love, casts men into unreality.

Yet as has frequently been noted, Conrad is not a political novelist in any simple sense and we do not expect a clear-cut political irony. *Under Western Eyes* presents politics and its institutions as shelters or connections that bear vitally upon private relationships. The Russian horror that voids Razumov's reality and imprisons him in irony works to legitimate the shelter of Western culture. Or rather, this is how, given Conrad's often expressed views on Russia, one might expect the narrative irony to function. The expectation, however, is frustrated by the spate of mutually canceling ironies that pervades the novel. The dramatic immediacy of Russian negations in parts one and four makes Western shelter into an irrelevant artifice. And Conrad seems to intend this effect. It is understandable that Razumov, at odds with himself and the world, should find Geneva "odious—oppressively odious—in its unsuggestive finish: the very perfection of mediocrity attained at last after centuries of toil and culture" (p. 203). But the function of the narrator's repeated sardonic comments, his insistence upon the city's "air of hypocritical respectability and of inexpressible dreariness" (p. 332), is far from clear. Schwartz notes that the language teacher's "querulous attitude to Geneva has troubled critics because that city's orderliness and preoccupation with private life appear to mirror his own standards."[7] Arguing for the centrality of the teacher's moral education in the scheme of the novel, Schwartz comments that the "narrator continually tests and redefines qualities that he associates with Russia and Geneva until, finally, he establishes the *moral* superiority of Western life."[8] Such superiority would be the tenor of the metaphor that the numerous ironic vehicles and situations pervert. Yet for all Conrad's empathic concern for the stark, denuding truth of "*cosas de Russia,*" the question posed by the political ironies is not one of superiority—which is never in doubt—but of the very possibility of moral meaning in a world that contains the fact of Russia. The narrator's irony about Genevan democracy is troubling enough in itself. When we see it, not as an element in a given, partially unreliable character, but as a recurrent and intensifying attitude to all illusions and complacencies of moral shelter—a response evident both in Marlow's narratives and in *Nostromo* and *The Secret Agent*—then the ironic scheme of *Under Western Eyes* risks association with the negation that Sophia Antonovna rebukes and with the "naive and hopeless cynicism" with which the narrator charges Russia.

The force of Razumov's story develops out of the absence of alternatives, meanings, and supporting values. Stranded between Haldin's terroristic idealism, which he loathes, and the autocracy that he knows will henceforth hold him suspect of involvement with Haldin, Razumov is stripped of what he considers the essential common denominator of a possible life: "to live without fear" (p. 69). He imagines himself arrested:

(p. 21)
> *shut up in a fortress, worried, badgered, perhaps ill-used. He saw himself deported by an administrative order, his life broken, ruined, and robbed of all hope. . . . Others had fathers, mothers, brothers, relations, connexions, to move heaven and earth on their behalf—he had no one. . . .*
>
> *He saw his youth pass away from him in misery and half starvation—his strength give way, his mind become an abject thing.*

Like numbers of other early modern protagonists, Razumov finds himself cut off from traditional structures of meaning and confronted with an unprecedented reality. Like others, he reacts by clinging despairingly to what once seemed stable truths. He will balk fate by turning Haldin over to the authority of his parent land. "Betray. A great word. What is betrayal? They talk of a man betraying his country, his friends, his sweetheart. There must be a moral bond first. All a man can betray is his conscience. And how is my conscience engaged here; by what bond of common faith, of common conviction, am I obliged to let that fanatical idiot drag me down with him?" (pp. 37–38). Most critics agree that the decision to inform on Haldin is the moral crux of the novel: that the bond to which Razumov is blind is the hidden tenor of his ironic fate. Razumov's reasoning is specious and his betrayal of Haldin on the basis of such reasoning even more of a crime against human trust than Jim's desertion. Yet both in its definition of Razumov's situation and in its empathic identification with his sensations, the narrative refuses any alternative to his act.

(p. 39)
> *Razumov longed desperately for a word of advice, for moral support. Who knows what true loneliness is—not the conventional word, but the naked terror? To the lonely themselves it wears a mask. The most miserable outcast hugs some memory or some illusion. Now and then a fatal conjunction of events may lift the veil for an instant. For an instant only. No human being could bear a steady view of moral solitude without going mad.*
> *Razumov had reached that point of vision.*

The fatality that has befallen Razumov charges him to do anything to achieve any kind of connection with others. To demand that the student in his naked terror exercise moral judgment—the kind of ethical balancing permitted by Western liberty—is to ask for an unthinkable heroic strength. The act has no content: only necessity. In his extremity, Razumov can veer from betrayal to absolute friendship. He suddenly wants to rush into his room and confess to Haldin: "to pour out a full confession in passionate words that would stir the whole being of that man to its innermost depths; that would end in embraces and tears; in an incredible fellowship of souls—such as the world had never seen. It was sublime!" (p. 40). In the utter loneliness of the breakdown of Razumov's life there is no distinction between betraying and embracing the assassin.

As so often in Conrad, an average man is thrust into a superlative situation. Though Razumov's nature is far fuller than Jim's, Nostromo's, or Winnie's, he too recalls those limited protagonists of naturalistic fiction who are victimized by vast forces beyond their control or ken. The terrific events that Conrad compacts into the first sixty pages of the novel sustain a chord of unbearable extremity. Razumov keeps trying to reinstate normality. Returning to his room where he must join the now-doomed Haldin, he attempts to view his fate as a mere passing inconvenience.

> *The exceptional could not prevail against the material contacts which make one day resemble another. To-morrow would be like yesterday.*
>
> *It was only on the stage that the unusual was outwardly acknowledged.*
>
> *"I suppose," thought Razumov, "that if I had made up my mind to blow my brains out on the landing I would be going up these stairs as quietly as I am doing it now. What's a man to do? What must be must be. Extraordinary things do happen. But when they have happened they are done with. Thus, too, when the mind is made up. That question is done with. And the daily concerns, the familiarities of our thought swallow it up—and the life goes on as before with its mysterious and secret sides quite out of sight, as they should be. Life is a public thing."*

(p. 54)

As the insistent truisms emphasize, these thoughts are a hollow effort at self-defense. The last comment—"Life is a public thing"—seems a fitting capstone to the flimsy edifice. The hope it contains is devastated by irony.

But Razumov's hope is Conrad's as well. The irony is entangled in the ramifications of the entire novel. Each of Conrad's novels pits private need against the bonds of public shelter; each employs irony to maintain at least a minimal faith in the viability of moral community in the face of human vulnerability and the anarchistic egotism to which mere personality is prone. No reader of Conrad would pause over the reliability of Razumov's comment or of the narrator's earlier statement that "a man's real life is that accorded to him in the thoughts of other men." Increasingly, Conrad's novels portray such reality as a faith rather than a fact, but the faith—even in the minimal form of those London masses that ridicule the terrorist's annihilating dream—is a central fact of Conrad's irony. In Razumov's Russian story, however, the quixotic and paradoxical orchestration of irony as a shelter against anarchy becomes a jarring alternation of remembered harmonies, silences, and horrid noise. Fidelity, devotion, service to a moral bond: these Conradian values start to seem empty platitudes reverberating without real meaning in the simple negation of Russia. The narrator's moral superiority and balanced viewpoint are true values, but they seem bland and hollow when forced to explain the outrageous context out of which Razumov and the exiled Russians emerge: "I suppose one must be a Russian to understand Russian simplicity, a terrible corroding simplicity in which mystic phrases clothe a naïve and hopeless cynicism. I think sometimes that the psychological secret of the profound difference of that people consists in this, that they detest life, the irremediable life of the earth as it is, whereas we westerners cherish it with perhaps an equal exaggeration of its sentimental value" (p. 104).

The nihilism that is Russia takes over from the exceptional events—storms, shipwrecks, revolutions, bombs—that violate normality and shelter and force character back upon its own resources. Like several of Conrad's other novels, *Under Western Eyes* was originally conceived as a novella. The action is characteristic of a genre that pursues the ramifications of an "unprecedented event" and often, as in works as different as Kleist's *Michael Kohlhaas* and James's *The Turn of the Screw*, carries its drama to or beyond the threshold of the supernatural.[9] Haldin's assassination of Mr. de P——and his violation of Razumov's life are expressions of Conrad's unprecedented event: Russia. The force of Razumov's parent nation, that "land of spectral ideas and disembodied aspirations" (p. 34), involves a cynicism about what the West takes to be reality. The unreal, the nightmarish, and the Gothic form a part of the student's being. Alongside what the Western eye can plainly see and Western words relate, there is, in Kermode's words, "another plot, misty, full of phantoms."[10] Like a harbored disease, this plot breaks forth in consequence of the wound to Razumov with which the action begins. The result is a sickness in the very fabric of moral and rational order: an outbreak of anarchy or entropy that calls all prescriptions and definitions into question. Conrad's concern with this secret subtext is based, not on ambivalence about the nature of

Western achievement, but on the suspicion that actuality may be diseased beyond the hope of any moral cure.

Razumov's fellow students, learning of Haldin's trust in him, take him as a silent partner of their ideals. "Again he experienced that sensation of his conduct being taken out of his hands by Haldin's revolutionary tyranny" (p. 82). At the same time, the apparent suspicions of the authorities mock Razumov's "real life." He receives an "official missive . . . from the superior direction of the police."

p. 83–84)
> He stared in dreary astonishment at the absurdity of his position. He thought with a sort of dry, unemotional melancholy; three years of good work gone, the course of forty more perhaps jeopardized—turned from hope to terror, because events started by human folly link themselves into a sequence which no sagacity can foresee and no courage can break through. Fatality enters your rooms while your landlady's back is turned; you come home and find it in possession bearing a man's name, clothed in flesh. . . . And it is all over. You cannot shake it off any more. It will cling to you for ever. Neither halter nor bullet can give you back the freedom of your life and the sanity of your thought.

Called to an interview with the police operative Councillor Mikulin, Razumov inveighs against his unprecedented fate. "To what is intelligible I can submit. But I protest against this comedy of persecution. The whole affair is becoming too comical altogether for my taste. A comedy of errors, phantoms, and suspicions. It's positively indecent . . ." (p. 99; Conrad's ellipsis). Finally, furious at not being able to lay Haldin's ghostly interference with his life, Razumov cries out that he is going "To retire—simply to retire." To which Mikulin quietly responds: "Where to?" (p. 99).

Razumov is a Russian Everyman: an impossible conjunction, since the exceptional negates any common life. During his first interview with Mikulin, he conjures up or perhaps really sees "some dark print of the Inquisition on the office wall." He records in the journal that the narrator is editing "a remarkably dream-like experience of anguish at the circumstance that there was no one whatever near the pale and extended figure [in the print]. The solitude of the racked victim was particularly horrible to behold. The mysterious impossibility to see the face, he also notes, inspired a sort of terror. All these characteristics of an ugly dream were present" (p. 88). The print images Razumov's situation. Solitude for Conrad is always a ghostly, blurred state. But in a novel that refers to sight in its title and is written by an author whose vocation is to make us see, the impossibility of seeing the protagonist's true face suggests the nightmarish irony of a central facelessness. An analogous irony darkens Marlow's account of Kurtz and Jim. In *Heart of Darkness*, when the stolid listeners are challenged to see—"Do you see him? Do you see the story? Do you see anything?"—the frame narrator observes: "It had become so pitch dark that we listeners could hardly see one another" (pp. 82–83). Kurtz and then Jim exist within an equivocal penumbra. But Razumov's drama is very nearly opaque. His reality ruptured, his vision distorted by hallucinations of Haldin and the drunken driver Ziemianitch, he has lost his story and himself in the pitch darkness of that Russia where, as Sophia Antonovna puts it, one lies "lapped up in evils, watched over by beings that are worse than ogres, ghouls, and vampires" (p. 254).

In such a state, Mikulin's "Where to?" is a truly ghoulish challenge. Ugly dreams spawn ugly answers, and Razumov has no apparent recourse but to seek visibility in invisibility, to embrace unreality as his reality. His ghostliness is intensified by the fact that we learn only at the beginning of the last part that he has accepted Mikulin's proposal and become a double agent spying out the secrets of the exiled revolutionaries who inhabit Geneva's *Petite Russie*. Arriving mysteriously in the city in part two, Razumov is placed directly before the language teacher's Western eyes. But the Genevan setting simply juxtaposes Dostoevskian extremity with the quiet precincts of a Turgenev. The scorn with which the pale prettiness, stale democracy, and Rousseauean temper of Geneva are presented compounds unreality. Just as the Congo flows into the estuary of the Thames, so anarchistic absurdity contaminates civilized banality. In *The Secret Agent*, Conrad's narrative irony mediates between the terroristic Professor on the one hand and the social superficiality, bumbling police, and uncharming lumpenproletariat on the other. In Razumov's story, no reliable perspective or voice controls the competing ironies.

The "respectable and passionless abode of democratic liberty" (p. 357) lies far apart from the indecent, passionate drama. No Genevans figure importantly in the action. The cast is made up exiles: Haldin's mother and sister, the squabbling nest of revolutionaries, and of course the English narrator. The thinness and instability of the background combine with the displaced human environment to underscore one of Conrad's recurrent concerns: the ironies of exile and of translation. Editing Razumov's story, the language teacher confronts the enormous task of translating "a Russian story for Western ears, which . . . are not attuned to certain notes of cynicism and cruelty, of moral negation, and even of moral distress already silenced at our end of Europe" (pp. 163–64). The narrator must both subvert our complacency and protect us from the moral contagion of his subject. His undertaking recalls Marlow's. But Razumov's nightmare demands a quite different narrative strategy. Marlow's ambiguous identification with a Kurtz or a Jim would be inappropriate. Conrad intends Marlow to be an uncomfortable presence. Razumov's story requires a more sheltering voice.

(p.3)
> To begin with I wish to disclaim the possession of those high gifts of imagination and expression which would have enabled my pen to create for the reader the personality of the man who called himself, after the Russian custom, Cyril son of Isidor—Kirylo Sidorovitch—Razumov.
>
> If I have ever had these gifts in any sort of living form they have been smothered out of existence a long time ago under a wilderness of words. Words, as is well known, are the great foes of reality. I have been for many years a teacher of languages. It is an occupation which at length becomes fatal to whatever share of imagination, observation, and insight an ordinary person may be heir to.

Opening with so blatant an advertisement of ordinariness, the narrative of Razumov's egregious fate embarks at once on irony.

The teacher's self-effacement approaches the limitations that Ford Madox Ford will portray in the baffled Dowell who narrates *The Good Soldier*. In part, of course, Conrad's strategy is traditional. The dull, conventional views of Lockwood and Nelly Dean help arouse sympathy for the absolutism of Emily Brontë's Catherine and Heathcliff. Guerard argues that the teacher's obtuseness creates sympathy for those afflicted by Russia's absolutism.[11] But this sympathy is compromised by its Western nurture: "It is not for us, the staid lovers calmed by the possession of a conquered liberty, to condemn without appeal the fierceness of thwarted desire" (p. 164). The narrator blunts the danger of fierceness, but he also dissipates the reality of desire. The prefatory statements seem to predict that a story such as Kurtz's is to be told by a narrator more akin to the Intended than to Marlow. This is not to argue that the "sensitivity and responsiveness" upon which Schwartz insists are of questionable worth.[12] The teacher's value as a narrator arises precisely from the combination of a kind of practical obtuseness with the civility, sensibility, and moral superiority that Conrad associates with women. As many critics have contended, the choice of a feminine temper to narrate a nightmare version of masculine engagement courts irony. But Conrad accepts the challenge because he now believes that only the ideal feminine truths at the heart of Western culture are capable of enduring and perhaps deflecting the fierceness of Russian cynicism.

The narrator begins by associating himself with the distrust of words shared by so many of Conrad's women, from Jewel to Winnie. "To a teacher of languages there comes a time when the world is but a place of many words and man appears a mere talking animal not much more wonderful than a parrot" (p. 3). "The Russians' extraordinary love of words" is an extreme instance of the futility of speech; they talk with such enthusiasm, with such "sweeping abundance that, as in the case of very accomplished parrots, one can't defend oneself from the suspicion that they really understand what they say" (p. 4). Razumov's journal itself, "the strange human document" that has come into the teacher's hands, is introduced under the key signature of this suspicion: "It would be idle to inquire why Mr. Razumov has left this record behind him. It is inconceivable that he should have wished any human eye to see it. A mysterious impulse of human nature comes into play here. . . . There must be a wonderful soothing power in mere words since so many men have used them for self-communion. Being myself a quiet individual I take it that what men are really after is some form or perhaps only some formula of peace" (pp. 4–5).

The wordplay that derives *formula* from *form* in disregard of the contradiction harks back to the defensive games that the narrative of *The Secret Agent* plays with language. At the same time it suggests one of the ironies—half-intended, half-unwanted—involved in the choice of a narrator who must express through the formulas of mere words the superior, sheltering form of feeling. The teacher's distrust of language is not quite the secret modernist message that Fleishman and Kermode discover in the text.[13] It is part of a conscious effort to locate Western moral truth in a realm proof against the vagaries of speech. Razumov's story will demand that the narrator exercise his protective editorial task upon material as appalling as that which confronts Marlow in Jewel's dread. But like Jim's clergyman father or the complacently optimistic "Fussy Joe" Mitchell, the narrator is essentially allied with the moral equivalent to our "sunny conveniences"; like women and children, he knows little of the ambivalence implicit in Marlow's narratives. A jocular, often querulous satiric tone—evident in the comments on Geneva, on Peter Ivanovitch, on Razumov, and most unsettlingly in the distrust of language—is a disturbing substitute for Marlow's elastic yet forceful ironies. Petty sarcasms must offset the irony of a fundamental lack of an ironic temper.

In a sense, of course, the narrator's personality and orientation carry to an extreme the basic hope of Conrad's impressionism: to go beyond words in order to make us see and feel. But Conrad's goal involves the self-consciousness of a cultural extension of romantic irony: literary impressionism must achieve the "lie too subtle to be found on earth" that Marlow considers the only possible alleviation of Jewel's nakedness. Employing the sights, decent responses, and feelings that are more real than words, Conrad's art can approximate the moral refuge that is the West's unique fiction and true achievement. The very obtuseness that permits the narrator, despite his many disclaimers, to believe he can narrate the negation beyond his culture's shelter precludes romantic irony. In so doing, it invites both situational and cosmic ironies. The teacher seeks "some key-word . . . that could stand at the back of all the words covering the pages, a word which, if not truth itself, may perchance hold truth enough to help the moral discovery which should be the object of every tale" (p. 67). No account of developing moral superiority can overcome the unselfconscious incongruity between this quest for a key word and the repeated distrust of mere words. Conrad's own awareness of the paradoxical situation of fiction is not in doubt. But the irony involved in the choice of a narrator of decent moral sensibility rather than ironic temper spreads out to compromise not just the teacher but the moral discovery his tale demands.

The teacher's personality does little to abate the force of the hallucinating concatenation of events leading to Razumov's interview with Mikulin. However, in the Genevan sections of the novel the narrator's voice and temperament become vital components of the drama he reports. The tame representative of Western sentiments becomes the point at which the half-opposing aspirations of Conrad's irony intersect. The protective function of irony collides with the suspicion of superficiality that Conrad associates with protection. The teacher's struggle to translate and order the entropic Russian story falls away from Marlow's heroic enterprise because the person who must do the translating is aligned with the faithful feelings that require shelter. As the perversion of Victor Haldin's heroic spirit into murderousness reveals, in Russia, the land of cynical negation and moral absurdity "where virtues themselves fester into crimes" (p. 356), no form of the masculine activism that Conrad transmutes into a Marlow or an Assistant Commissioner can avail. The fact of Russia necessitates revolutionary action. But the revolution that Conrad envisages must itself be of a radically new type. Unprecedented circumstances exact unprecedented measures. With extreme ambivalence, Conrad moves toward the faith in the force of women that Rilke expresses in *Malte Laurids Brigge* and Lawrence in *The Rainbow*. As I have shown, the teacher's nature fits him to narrate this revolution. But here too we find an undercutting irony. For the narrator resembles and exalts a model of feminine value much like that portrayed in the Intended and Emilia Gould. The revolutionary feminine absolutism that can counter Russian nihilism recalls Antonia Avellanos and Linda Viola, figures Conrad admires and yet keeps at a distance. Absolutism may harbor the fierceness of a Winnie Verloc. The relation among traditional heroic virtues, the decency of moral shelter, and female force is equivocal. And the narrator's equivocation compromises the one hope that the novel permits.

The Genevan action of Razumov's story revolves around women: Victor Haldin's sister, "Miss Haldin—Nathalie, caressingly Naltalka" (p. 100), will be the center of a gallery including her mother, Tekla, and Sophia Antonovna. Singly and collectively, these four press the qualities Conrad vests in women into Russian extremity. Mrs. Haldin, embodying the fearful vulnerability portrayed in the Intended, Jewel, Mrs. Gould, and Winnie, is the most conventionally conceived of the group. But her loss and mournful decline are more rendingly, even melodramatically unadulterated than those experienced by her predecessors. "It is strange to think that, I won't say liberty, but the mere liberalism of outlook which for us is a matter of words, of ambitions, of votes (and if of feeling at all, then of the sort of feeling which leaves our deepest affections untouched) may be for other beings very much like ourselves and living under the same sky, a heavy trial of fortitude, a matter of tears and anguish and blood" (p. 318). Mrs. Haldin's anguish announces the absolute condition of sentiment beyond the pale. She "was one of those natures, rare enough, luckily, . . . [that provokes] both terror and pity." If Russia transforms the victimizing force of negation into the final authority of its cynical Realpolitik, then Mrs. Haldin raises vulnerability into an archetype of untranslatable bereftness that marshalls the whole dignity of human feeling.

> 338—
> *She did not move. . . . outside there was only the night sky harbouring a thunder-cloud, and the town indifferent and hospitable in its cold, almost scornful, toleration—a respectable town of refuge to which all these sorrows and hopes were nothing. Her white head was bowed.*

> *The thought that the real drama of autocracy is not played on the great stage of politics came to me as, fated to be a spectator, I had this other glimpse behind the scenes, something more profound than the words and gestures of the public play. . . . It was more than Rachel's inconsolable mourning, it was something deeper, more inaccessible in its frightful tranquillity.*

Supreme pain mocks formulas for refuge. Mrs. Haldin's suffering is an outrageous call. But the town is indifferent, the narrator a spectator, and Razumov too agonized in his duplicity. Such plangent misery, moreover, exacts an ungainly absolutism of response. Only the indecent fierceness of a Tekla, the maltreated companion of Madame de S——— and scorned secretary of Peter Ivanovitch, might promise the necessary strength. As a child, seeing how her father's work in the Ministry of Finance plunged the innocent into wretchedness and injustice, Tekla turned her back on her family and vowed her life to a war on ministries. "Devoid of all comeliness of feature and complexion as the most miserable beggar is of money" (p. 232), she lives only in "her starving, grotesque, and pathetic devotion" (p. 234). In Geneva her hateful employers have degraded her vocation and "decomposed her fidelity" (p. 235). She emerges before Razumov as another of the specters that haunt his unreality: a sad nonentity whose anonymity seems a threadbare parody of his own. "I have no use for a name, and have almost forgotten it myself. . . . You may call me Tekla, then. My poor Andrei [the first of the broken victims she has served] called me so. I was devoted to him. He lived in wretchedness and suffering and died in misery. That is the lot of all us Russians, nameless Russians. There is nothing else for us, and no hope anywhere. . . . Unless all these people with names are done away with . . ." (pp. 235–36). Razumov's attitude toward the figure of what M. D. Zabel calls "cowed humility" is friendly but dismissive.[14] Yet at the end of the novel, after Nikita has burst his eardrums and the unheard streetcar shattered his body, it is this nameless force of devotion, this desolate quintessence of a single feminine strength, that sweeps Razumov up from his hospital ward and carries him back to his homeland. "He was crippled, ill, getting weaker every day, and Tekla the

Samaritan tended him unwearied with pure joy of unselfish devotion. There was nothing in that task [for her] to become disillusioned about" (p. 379).

Just as the narrator's comments on Razumov in Geneva combine irritation at the corroding cynicism of a Russian nature with deep feeling for what seems a Russian plight, so the portrait of Tekla conjoins sympathy, admiration, and a radically distancing satiric condescension. Like other Russians, the Samaritan is humanly real and morally fantastic. But the appalling fantasy seems the only response to the glimpse of something more profound than the words of our public play. The suggestion is further complicated in the portrait of Sophia Antonovna, the only at all appealing member of Peter Ivanovitch's inner circle. The "woman revolutionist" (p. 253) incarnates the derangement of male and female qualities and spheres of action. She herself is well aware that conventional definitions no longer suffice. In her long conversation with Razumov she insists upon his tendency to repeat the errors she associates with men; she rails at his "masculine nature" (p. 246), his "petty masculine standards" (p. 248), and his "masculine cowardice" (p. 250). Like Tekla, she has become what she is through hatred of "the great social iniquity of the system resting on unrequited toil and unpitied sufferings" (p. 262). The horror of Russian injustice is the work of men. From the moment that the example of her father's life taught her this, "I was a revolutionist." In her, compassion becomes vengeance. Anything else would be "a shameful thing like some kinds of life. . . . The subservient, submissive life. Life? No! Vegetation on the filthy heap of iniquity which the world is. Life, Razumov, not to be vile must be a revolt—a pitiless protest—all the time" (p. 260). The "revolutionary pilgrimage" (p. 264) to which she brings all her force of feeling, of sensitivity, and intuition lays bare "the secret, not of everlasting youth, but of everlasting endurance" (p. 261). The "respected, trusted, and influential Sophia Antonovna, whose word had such a weight in the 'active' section of every party . . . was much more representative than the great Peter Ivanovitch. Stripped of rhetoric, mysticism, and theories, she was the true spirit of destructive revolution" (p. 261).

This spirit is truer than words. Contrasted both with Western complacency and with those like Razumov in whom Russian vileness nurtures a "disease of perversity" (p. 253), Sophia Antonovna has the power to act. She opposes belief to cynicism; she pits an "uncompromising sense of necessity and justice" against Razumov's pessimistic conviction that in "this world of men nothing can be changed" (p. 261). The acuity of her nature and her faith frighten Razumov, whose self-protective reactions seem to parallel the narrator's desire for some distance from such "invincible vigour of revolt" (p. 263). As with Tekla, the teacher is appalled by the power of "strong individualism" (p. 264) behind the spectacle of devoted flatness, of feminine force etched bare by cruel reality. No less than Razumov, these women have been violated in the most vulnerable truth of their natures. They have emerged intensified to the point of archetype. Razumov vacillates in pain, a sport of horror susceptible to irony and moral judgment. The women seem to emerge as specters from a realm beyond the reach of irony and conventional standards. Yet part of what the narrator responds to involves, not irony, but simple humanity. However strong in feeling, endurance, and revolt, both Tekla and Sophia Antonovna are maimed; their single-minded strength is a symptom of the dessicating Russian disease that wastes the rightness of being Conrad idealizes in women. The two women are warnings quite as much as they are exemplars. Both are minor figures in the action; both exist as comments on the possibilities dramatized in far greater fullness and far more complexly in the portrait of Nathalie Haldin.

Razumov is a high average of masculine character; Nathalie is presented as an especially promising example of womanhood. Though as Moser notes, she appears in person in far fewer scenes than Conrad originally intended, most critics have responded to her vibrancy. Few would agree that "she remains little more than a speaker of noble sentiments, with a frank, healthy walk and a virile handclasp."[15] Clearly, however, being Russian in a book that presents Russian humanity as corroded in its essence, she too is damaged. Her personality is shaped by "life as it was made for her by the political conditions of her country. She faced cruel realities, not morbid imaginings of her own making" (p. 117). These realities make private feeling a public creed; they exact a starker hope than the subtle alchemy of material interests into moral culture to which Emilia Gould devotes her life. Nathalie's worship of her brother joins intense love to political faith; she shares his belief "in the power of a people's will to achieve anything": "Of course the will must be awakened, inspired, concentrated. . . . That is the true task of real agitators. One has got to give up one's life to it. The degradation of servitude, the absolutistic lies must be uprooted and swept out. Reform is impossible. There is nothing to reform. There is no legality, there are no institutions. There are only arbitrary decrees. There is only a handful of cruel—perhaps blind—officials against a nation" (p. 133). Her nurture has taught her the public meaning of truth and reality: a meaning, she explains to her friend the language teacher, almost willfully obscured in his world. Westerners, those who have "made a bargain with fate . . . so much liberty for so much hard cash," "shrink from the idea of revolutionary action for those you think well of as if it were something—how shall I say it—not quite decent" (p. 134). For all his personal sympathy, the narrator does of course find the public idea indecent. True idealists may begin a revolution, "but it passes away from them. They are not the leaders of a revolution. They are its victims: the victims of disgust, of disenchantment—often of remorse. Hopes grotesquely betrayed, ideals caricatured—that is the definition of revolutionary success" (pp. 134–35). Soured, maimed, or perverted feeling is the sad aftermath of all revolutionism. Such opinions are close to those repeatedly expressed in Conrad's own statements on the subject. Yet Nathalie's unanswerable rejoinder stands as the epigraph that Conrad chooses for *Under Western Eyes*: "I would take liberty from any hand as a hungry man would snatch at a piece of bread." "True progress," she adds, "must begin after" (p. 135).

Nathalie's words distill the horror enacted in Razumov's story and the sole hope that has made Tekla and Sophia Antonovna what they are. The hunger for which she speaks cannot be mitigated by ambiguity, disinterested wisdom, or irony. Unlike the other women, however, Nathalie is fresh, young, and attractive. If the creed she proclaims seems little more than a naive string of noble sentiments, it is in part because she is "so true, so honest, but so dangerously inexperienced! Her unconsciously lofty ignorance of the baser instincts of mankind left her disarmed before her own impulses" (pp. 142–43). Her vibrant ingenuousness is perfectly matched to her brother's ideal formulas: "Our dear one told me once to remember that men serve always something greater than themselves—the idea" (p. 352). But just as Razumov's experience casts doubt on the premise that man's true life lies in the thoughts of others, so this naïveté, which condenses the devoted innocence Conrad portrays in his good women, compromises Nathalie's version of a premise central to Conrad's previous fiction. Assassination, after all, is the practical expression of her dear one's idea. The full-bodied feminine idealism that speaks for the idea of revolution is in its way as alien to conventional womanhood as Jewel's denuding fear. Nathalie's nature has been "robbed arbitrarily of its natural lightness and joy, overshadowed by an un-European despotism; [hers is] a terribly sombre youth given over to the hazards of a furious strife between equally ferocious antagonisms" (p. 319). The charming girl that the somewhat Prufrockian teacher almost loves never quite exists. At the end of the novel, after the loss of her mother and of the hope she has transferred from her brother to Razumov, she disappears altogether into a life of obscure service in the hinterlands of Russia. "There was no longer any Natalia Haldin, because she had completely ceased to think of herself. It was a great victory, a characteristically Russian exploit in self-suppression" (p. 375).

A conviction of waste, victimization, and ghostly abstraction transforms the narrator's more than affectionate admiration into sardonic irony. Nathalie becomes yet another instance of Russia's voiding of all decency and value: another piece of human flotsam in the maelstrom of negation. We remember the narrator's early comment that, in its "secret readiness to abase itself in suffering, the spirit of Russia is the spirit of cynicism. It informs the declarations of her statesmen, the theories of her revolutionists, and the mystic vaticinations of prophets to the point of making freedom look like a form of debauch, and the Christian virtues themselves appear actually indecent" (p. 67). The self-sacrificing, faithful feelings of an

Emilia Gould or a Winnie Verloc are no longer the civilizing gifts of true women, but an indecent destitution of self.

Yet the irony that seems the message of Nathalie's sentiments and life is, like so much else in the novel, itself complicated by other ironies. The narrator's bias toward conventional feminine action is of dubious reliability at best. His own version of woman's sentiments makes him simultaneously a source for and a mocker of the values around which the novel ambiguously hovers. More immediately, the irony surrounding Nathalie is interwoven with that contained in Razumov, who is after all the major focus of the novel. Nathalie appears as often under Razumov's Russian eyes as under the teacher's Western gaze. To Razumov she will be the sole avenue of escape from the moral claustrophobia that dominates his Genevan double life. "The choking fumes of falsehood had taken him by the throat—the thought of being condemned to struggle on and on in that tainted atmosphere without the hope of ever renewing his strength by a breath of fresh air" (p. 269). In the final scene of the third part, Razumov seeks refuge and air on a tiny island "where the exiled effigy of the author of the *Social Contract* sat enthroned" (p. 291). He writes his reports to Mikulin and his secret diary in the shadow of an irony that orchestrates exile, justice, social reason, and liberal sentiment. His only company is the murmuring of the current. It "occurred to him that this was about the only sound he could listen to innocently, and for his own pleasure, as it were. Yes, the sound of water, the voice of the wind—completely foreign to human passions. All the other sounds of this earth brought contamination to the solitude of a soul" (p. 291). The passage stresses the motifs—solitude, immobility, and sound—that will dominate the novel's final movement. At the end, Conrad will deliver Razumov to a paradoxically plangent silence: a reality beyond words, perhaps beyond what is now termed narratability. If this silence is to have any moral meaning, that meaning must reside in whatever form or perhaps only formula of peace Razumov can rescue from his experience of Nathalie.

The last part of *Under Western Eyes* takes us back to the abyss in which Razumov founders after he informs on Haldin. Existence is given over to ghosts and to rage. Razumov flies into tantrums like a child whose dearest safeties have been ripped away. "And all this was Haldin, always Haldin—nothing but Haldin—everywhere Haldin: a moral spectre infinitely more effective than any visible apparition of the dead" (pp. 299–300). He wants to "creep in somewhere": to flee his feeling of "unnamed and despairing dread, mingled with an odious sense of humiliation" (p. 301).

(p. 303) *And again, but with a different mental accent, Razumov said to himself, "I am young. Everything can be lived down." At that moment he was crossing the room slowly, intending to sit down on the sofa and try to compose his thoughts. But before he had got so far everything abandoned him—hope, courage, belief in himself, trust in men. . . . Rest, work, solitude, and the frankness of intercourse with his kind were alike forbidden to him. Everything was gone. His existence was a great cold blank, something like the enormous plain of the whole of Russia levelled with snow and fading gradually on all sides into shadows and mists.*

Razumov is emptied by injustice, anguish, and negation into the human condition to which Tekla, Sophia Antonovna, and finally Nathalie vow to devote their lives. In this state he returns to Mikulin's office to accept the offer of a double agent's life "with the eagerness of a pursued person welcoming any sort of shelter" (p. 304).

Razumov becomes the protagonist of what Russia means. His reality is unreality; his existence, an accursed, ghoulish fantasy. Our sharpened sense of the agony that Razumov carries with him to Geneva both counterposes the narrator's irritated judgments and accompanies Razumov's desperate efforts to escape back into reality. His first attempt leads him at long last to Mrs. Haldin; arriving like "a haunted somnambulist," he tells her his false version of her son's final hours. But the "phantom's mother consumed with grief and white as a ghost" (p. 340) is beyond hearing or believing anything. She only intensifies his pain and unbearable unsubstantiality. Stepping out of her room, he meets Nathalie and the teacher. Since his first interview with the young woman, she too "has been haunting him" (p. 342). Yet she also seems to suggest a hopeful magic. To the narrator, the man and woman appear "like two people becoming conscious of a spell that has been lying on them" (p. 345). Razumov has "the air of a man who is listening to a strain of music rather than to articulated speech. . . . [He was] motionless, as if under the spell of suggestive sound" (p. 348). The true encounter takes place far from those words that "are the great foes of reality." The suggestiveness of course is in part that of the traditional charm of love. But a Russian black magic perverts this feeling as well as all others. The very attraction Razumov feels bears with it the temptation to a betrayal even worse than that of Nathalie's brother.

Nathalie becomes the only conceivable answer to Mikulin's "Where to?" During Victor Haldin's few hours in Razumov's room, he had spoken of his sister in words that, as Razumov now tells her, "meant that there is in you no guile, no deception, no falsehood, no suspicion—nothing in your heart that could give you a conception of a living, acting, speaking lie, if ever it came your way. That you are a predestined victim. . . . Ha! what a devilish suggestion!" (p. 349; Conrad's ellipsis). Just one more lie spoken to Nathalie and Razumov will be safe forever; the revolutionists will never again question his bond with Victor Haldin if he is married to Victor's sister. As in the opening episode of the betrayal that begins Razumov's unprecedented story, so now in the scene that must grant the story a moral climax the need for action is intolerably overwrought. "Do you know why I came to you? It is simply because there is no one anywhere in the whole great world I could go to. Do you understand what I say? Not one to go to. Do you conceive the desolation of the thought—no one—to—go—to?" (pp. 353–54). For Razumov, Nathalie is refuge, the idea, the silver medal he had once hoped would win him an acknowledged name and real identity. For Nathalie, the need is almost equally desperate. Those she loves—the brother whose faith had sheltered and given meaning to her being; the mother whose dedication had sustained her—are dead or dying. Razumov appears as the sole heir to hope. He bears "the only name to be found in the correspondence between brother and sister. . . . the only name uttered in all the dream-talk of a future to be brought about by a revolution" (p. 165).

In the interview that follows, Razumov, the brother's nemesis, almost gives way to the temptation to win the sister to his falsehood. Only at the final instant does he draw back and implicitly confess the truth that he was Victor's betrayer. As he writes later in his diary, Nathalie's "purity" saves him "from ignominy, from ultimate undoing." "Your light! your truth! I felt that I must tell you that I had ended by loving you. And to tell you that I must first confess. Confess, go out—and perish" (p. 361). Guerard finds the confession of cynicism and evil that in the diary account counterpoints the avowal of love to be "rhetorical, arbitrary, untrue."[16] Certainly, both the evil and the love are expressed with a vehement straightforwardness that distorts the irreducible ambiguity of need, despair, and hope previously achieved in the portrait of Razumov. Yet if the interview is to be charged with Razumov's starkest glimpse of emptiness and the unbearable movement toward what Guerard calls his "triumph," then such rhetorical heightening is at least understandable. The cost of Razumov's falsehood to Nathalie is a paralysis of action, hope, and meaning that surely underscores the absolute stakes that have been raised. Nathalie, stricken, points "mournfully at the tragic immobility of her mother," which now seems her own fate. For the moment, Razumov too is frozen, standing "with an appalled expressionless tranquility," "as if rooted to the spot of his atrocious confession." Then, unconsciously carrying with him the veil that Nathalie has dropped, he rushes out. The teacher, always a spectator, starts to shout angrily after him, but is cut off by the sight of the young woman. "Shadows seemed to come and go in [her eyes] as if the steady flame of her soul had been made to vacillate at last in the cross-currents of poisoned air from the corrupted dark immensity claiming her for its own, where virtues themselves fester into crimes in the cynicism of oppression and revolt." "It is impossible to be more unhappy," she says; "I feel my heart becoming like ice" (pp. 355–56).

Nathalie and Razumov, valuable natures akin to the best of Western youth, are victims of a Russia that as we know Conrad abhors. Their fate is the novel's political message. Yet the poisonous land that paralyzes their being is also Conrad's fullest evocation of the darkness surrounding all the endeavors of moral civilization. It is not Russia, after all, that accounts for the horror portrayed in Kurtz, Gentleman Brown, Mr. Verloc, and the Professor. Russia is not the source, but the institutionalization of the cosmic irony that mocks and opposes man's hopes. Nathalie and Razumov's homeland is the nemesis of the self-consciously articulated moral idea that Conrad's romantic irony would protect. Because Russia is the naturalistic expression of horror, however, because its race, moment, and milieu destroy all value and meaning, it must also contain the very essence of the cruel truths that moral culture must confront if it is to be any sort of viable shelter. Like many of Conrad's other novels, but more nakedly, *Under Western Eyes* develops around what Martin Swales, describing the German *Novelle*, terms a "hermenuetic gamble." The unprecedented situation that is Russia conveys a "set of experiences that would appear to conflict utterly with any notion of order or manageable interpretation." These experiences necessitate a narrative act of defense that will restore "an ordered and reliably interpreted human universe."[17] Conrad's novel repeats the tense gamble dramatized in Marlow's response to Kurtz. The fact of horror, and the need to know and acknowledge the truth it contains, is set against the ability to interpret the horror and to impose meaning upon it. For Razumov, the truth he loves in Nathalie's purity must be strong enough to give meaning to perdition.

Razumov's confession, like Raskolnikov's in *Crime and Punishment*, which seems to function in Conrad's imagination as a ghostly double of his own novel, is based as much on pride and chagrin as on contrition. In Dostoevsky's work, however, those to whom Raskolnikov grudgingly confesses represent a fallen, secular version of God's truth. The murderer's pride stands in the way of this truth. Razumov's pride is of a quite opposite kind. His inspiration, Nathalie's truth, combines purity and innocence with a belief in the necessity of revolution against injustice and misery. Razumov rushes from Nathalie to confess his responsibility for Victor Haldin's capture before the revolutionists assembled around Peter Ivanovitch. They "have the right on their side!—theirs is the strength of invisible powers. So be it. Only don't be deceived, Natalia Victorovna, I am not converted. Have I then the soul of a slave? No! I am independent—and therefore perdition is my lot" (pp. 361–62). A "puppet of his past," he enters the meeting at the very midnight hour during which he had betrayed Haldin. "I beg you to observe . . . that I had only to hold my tongue. To-day, of all days since I came amongst you, I was made safe [by the lie he almost told Nathalie], and to-day I made myself free from falsehood, from remorse—independent of every single being on this earth" (p. 368). According to many interpreters, Razumov's truth redeems something of his earlier falsehood; his act rescues moral freedom from deterministic horror. He is now fit to love Nathalie.

But the moral intention of the confession is a good deal clearer than the interwoven horror, melodrama, satire, and hope that govern the brief concluding sections of the novel. As an exemplary, almost symbolic rendition of the rescuing of moral independence from all that opposes it, Razumov may perform an errand of hope. Yet despite the narrator's caviling comments, we have lived the egotism of Razumov's anguish with overwhelming mimetic intimacy. And this intimacy continues into the account of the perdition awaiting Razumov after his confession. Just outside the meeting room, Nikita, "nicknamed Necator," a creature "so grotesque as to set town dogs barking" (pp. 266, 267), bursts Razumov's eardrums with his fists. "With his big, livid cheeks, his heavy paunch, bull neck, and enormous hands" (p. 367), Nikita seems less "the perfect flower of the terroristic wilderness" (p. ix) that is Russia, than the reduction to atrocity of the vileness of physical reality so prominently displayed in *The Secret Agent*. Nikita murders the sounds and words that express any life beyond the self. Razumov may achieve some interpretable triumph, but he does so at the cost of reality. He is now a ghost. "In this unearthly stillness his footsteps fell silent on the pavement, while a dumb wind drove him on and on, like a lost mortal in a phantom world ravaged by a soundless thunderstorm" (pp. 369–70). At the end of the third part "the sound of water, the voice of the wind" could be heard in innocence and with pleasure; all "other sounds of this earth brought contamination to the solitude of a soul" (p. 291). Now the soul may be pure, but the body is broken by the streetcar Razumov cannot hear. As he lies in the hospital, Tekla appears to claim this new object for her nameless devotion. "I am a relation. . . . This young man is a Russian, and I am his relation" (p. 371).

Razumov fades from sight into the invisibility of a freed soul. Mrs. Haldin dies. Nathalie is about to disappear like Razumov into Russia. The narrator visits her for a last time. "To my Western eyes she seemed to be getting farther and farther from me, quite beyond my reach now, but undiminished in the increasing distance" (p. 374). Since almost all of Conrad's earlier portraits of the truth invested in women are diminished by their tears, pathos, and pain, the qualities that the teacher now sees in Nathalie possess an unprecedented value. "Natalia Haldin looked matured by her open and secret experiences. . . . She gave me a new view of herself, and I marvelled at that something grave and measured in her voice, in her movements, in her manner. It was the perfection of collected independence. The strength of her nature had come to surface because the obscure depths had been stirred" (p. 373). When Winnie Verloc's obscure depths are quickened, she becomes first a murderer and then a suicide. Nathalie has become an interpreter: "My eyes are open at last and my hands are free now. As for the rest—which of us can fail to hear the stifled cry of our great distress? . . . I must own to you that I shall never give up looking forward to the day when all discord shall be silenced. Try to imagine its dawn! The tempest of blows and of execrations is over; all is still. . . . [Weary men] feel alone on the earth and gather close together. Yes, there must be bitter hours! But at last the anguish of hearts shall be extinguished in love" (pp. 376–77). "Love" is what the teacher calls "the last word of [Nathalie's] wisdom, a word so sweet, so bitter, so cruel sometimes. . . . It is hard to think that I shall never look any more into the trustful eyes of that girl—wedded to an invincible belief in the advent of loving concord springing like a heavenly flower from the soil of men's earth, soaked in blood, torn by struggles, watered with tears" (p. 377).

Nathalie's purity has from the beginning commanded her brother's, Razumov's and the narrator's profound allegiance. Now matured and strengthened, she speaks for the redemptive power of the crucial Conradian virtues that Sophia Antonovna proclaims to Razumov: for the saving instincts, faith, devotion, and action that forbid irony. Nathalie's valedictory is the prelude to the revolution that with Tekla and others like her she is about to undertake. She will bear a self resistant to irony, a life of feminine feeling tempered to the pitch of masculine action, into the homeland of irony. The teacher, with his decent sentiments and his empathy for the culture women incarnate, is the necessary spokesman for Nathalie's mission to men's earth. Yet he applauds Nathalie's light and truth rather than her newfound force. Such force embodies "a characteristically Russian exploit in self-suppression" (p. 374); it links the young woman with the deindividualizing, even grotesque absolutism of a Tekla and a Sophia. Nathalie's words are to be taken as beyond irony, while her very being is cast into irony. Set against the cruel and contradictory ironies of Russia and Russianness, Nathalie's last word seems as naked and vulnerable as Razumov was even before Victor Haldin violated his life: "as lonely in the world as a man swimming in the deep sea" (p. 10).

Words are the enemies of reality, and Nathalie's speech invites the charge of mere noble sentiments brought by Moser. Unlike Dr. Monygham in *Nostromo*, whose embittered cynicism protects Emilia Gould from irony and prepares our assent to her ideal truth, the language teacher and his sheltered, cultivated decencies, which work well to set off the horrid ironies of Razumov's story, do nothing to protect Nathalie's apotheosis of the sentiment of culture. Nathalie proclaims something approximating the purgatorial hope that takes over from infernal fact in the Epilogue to *Crime and Punishment*. But there is no unironic equivalent in *Under Western Eyes* to the truth of Christ that grants the new life Dostoevsky adumbrates. In Guerard's words, "Nathalie's vision of unity and her contempt for political parties are Russian, so too is her mystical vision of a time of concord."[18] Nothing less than Nathalie's extremity of hope and absolute dedication of self can counter the infernal specter of Russia. But the hope and dedication are themselves Russian. Nathalie's expression of the hope may be another example of "the Russians' extraordinary love of words." Her dedication may be another indecent and appalling example of Russia's transformation of virtues into crimes. Russia is the irresistible reality of the unreal; the field of black force that transforms everything into its opposite, into an irony beyond the reach of Conrad's ironic faith.

Unlike the Epilogue to Dostoevsky's novel or the enriching ambiguity with which Marlow surrounds his parting glimpse of Jim's equivocal reality, the few pages that serve as epilogue to *Under Western Eyes* only reinforce the painful sense of impasse: of hopes and fears that cancel each other and of the thwarting of interpretation. The woman revolutionary Sophia Antonovna returns two years later from Russia. The news she conveys with "a touch of enthusiasm" (p. 378) to the narrator is of course tainted by its source. Sophia's womanly insight and truth are distorted by horror and unreality. Her unreliability, however, is no greater than that of the baffled responses of the Western narrator who reports their encounter. Sophia tells of Nathalie's new life. The young woman is "sharing her compassionate labours between the horrors of overcrowded jails and the heartrending misery of bereaved homes." Nathalie "has a faithful soul, an undaunted spirit and an indefatigable body." She lives her nameless life of "good service" in a nameless town somewhere "in the centre" of Russia (p. 378). We learn no more. The tone with which the teacher passes on Sophia's furtive information is flat, almost grudging.

The final references to Razumov, whose unprecedented fate the narrative has attempted to clothe in the order and refuge of Western words, are similarly bleak and ambiguous. The teacher does "not even understand the motive" that leads Sophia Antonovna and other revolutionaries to visit the confessed and broken informer. She explains: "He is intelligent. He has ideas. . . . He talks well, too" (p. 379; Conrad's ellipsis). We are not told what, if anything, might distinguish these ideas and this talk from the Russian parroting we have been instructed to suspect. Even more confusing is Sophia's praise of Razumov's courage in striking out at "the ignominy of the existence before him" by confessing to Peter Ivanovitch's meeting. "There's character in such a discovery," she says (p. 380). At the time of his confession Razumov insisted that he was not converted to revolution: that he was independent, not a slave to ideas he detested. Has he now become a partisan, a voice of wisdom for the revolutionists? We are not told. From a Western point of view his selfhood seems to have been destroyed along with his falsehood. "Character" in Conrad is public achievement, but the definition has been eroded by the ironies of the narrative. Sophia adds that there is a degree of guilt behind the revolutionists' attention to Razumov. Nikita's vile act was performed without approval and Nikita himself has been unmasked as the most dastardly of double agents. Yet again this information seems almost random, without clear point. "And this story, too, I received without comment in my character of a mute witness of things Russian, unrolling their Eastern logic under my Western eyes" (p. 381).

Most perplexing of all is the emphasis accorded in this brief summing up to Peter Ivanovitch's fate. Nathalie's devotion to loving concord, Razumov's tragically earned "character," and Nikita's evil are place alongside the sardonic conclusion to the story of this revolutionary feminist. The juxtaposition underscores the question that has bothered many readers: why does Conrad devote so much of the energy of the middle sections of the novel to the bitterly sarcastic account of Peter Ivanovitch and his consort, the grotesque "harridan" Madame de S———? The teacher has presented the "heroic fugitive" as an insidious threat to Nathalie and her ideals. "All Europe was aware of the story of his life written by himself and translated into seven or more languages." Imprisoned as a conspirator in Russia, Peter Ivanovitch had escaped, dragging his still-fettered leg across the subcontinent. He was aided first by one woman and then, starving and reduced to near-bestiality, by another who discovered through "the insight of her feminine compassion . . . the man under the terrifying aspect of the monster." The girl helps him to free himself of his chains. "There are in his book whole pages of self-analysis whence emerges like a white figure from a dark confused sea the conviction of woman's spiritual superiority—his new faith confessed since in several volumes." In Geneva, Peter Ivanovitch preaches the "cult of the woman" and practices it "under the rites of his special devotion to the transcendental merits of a certain Madame de S———" (pp. 120–25). The narrator's vicious portrait combines the traits of Comrade Ossipon with suggestions of a mysterious and nasty psychological overlordship. But now we learn from Sophia Antonovna that the man was no match for his "painted, bedizened, dead-faced, glassy-eyed Egeria" (p. 161). Madame de S—— has died intestate. Her devotee receives nothing. He returns to Russia where he attaches himself to a peasant girl whom "he just simply adores." The teacher interjects scornfully: "I hope that she won't hesitate to beat him."

(p. 382)
> Sophia Antonovna got up and wished me good-bye, as though she had not heard a word of my impious hope; but, in the very doorway, where I attended her, she turned round for an instant, and declared in a firm voice—
> "Peter Ivanovitch is an inspired man."

Sophia's words conclude the novel, and cast the struggle to impose interpretative order into final disarray. Peter Ivanovitch is a brilliant satiric foil. As Moser writes, "Never did Conrad more effectively satirize his own tendency to sentimentalize women."[19] But in a book so fundamentally concerned with feminine strength and truth, more than satire is involved. Peter Ivanovitch becomes a damagingly ironic counterpoint to the endeavor to present women as a heroic hope. The irony attending the unpalatable feminist, possessing as it does the resonance attending a novel's last words, amplifies with corroding force the ambivalence toward women's meaning that will figure so irritatingly in Marlow's misogynous contribution to *Chance*, Conrad's next novel. Being Russian, Peter Ivanovitch of course perverts feminism. Yet the narrator mocks, not just the caricature, but the fragile faith it distorts. His petulant response is itself a perversion: an example of the male pusillanimity that Sophia rebukes in Razumov. Together, the fraudulence of the revolutionary feminist, the Western weakness of the teacher, and the enthusiastic inversion of the truth of words conveyed in the woman revolutionist's praise defeat any hope of stemming the horror that flows from beyond the pale. These separate shadows cohere into a cosmic darkness too black for Conrad's self-conscious ironic play of light and shadow, reality and ghostliness, moral faith and cynical fact. There is no narrative home for the artificing of faith, for the ironic strategies that might protect the truth that Marlow locates in the Intended: "that great and saving illusion that shone with an unearthly glow in the darkness" (p. 159). *Under*

Western Eyes, for all its rending sympathies and competing ironies, cannot finally reconstitute Marlow's ability to rebuild the enclave of belief after the deafening silence of Jewel's dread. The ordering virtue of that ironic art is, like Razumov, reduced to solitary words in a dead sea of silence.

Notes

Index

Notes

Introduction: A Choice of Ironies

1. Ian Watt, *Conrad in the Nineteenth Century* (Berkeley and Los Angeles: Univ. of California Press, 1979), pp. 175–79.
2. Cedric Watts, *The Deceptive Text* (Sussex: Harvester Press, 1984), p. 13.
3. Albert J. Guerard, *Conrad the Novelist* (New York: Atheneum, 1967), pp. 32–48.
4. Thomas Moser, *Joseph Conrad: Achievement and Decline* (Cambridge: Harvard Univ. Press, 1957), p. 79.
5. D. C. Muecke, *The Compass of Irony* (London: Methuen, 1969); idem, *Irony*, Critical Idiom Series, vol. 13 (London: Methuen, 1970); Wayne C. Booth, *A Rhetoric of Irony* (Chicago: Univ. of Chicago Press, 1974).
6. Jonathan Culler, *Flaubert: The Uses of Uncertainty* (Ithaca: Cornell Univ. Press, 1974), p. 211.
7. Muecke, *Irony*, p. 20.
8. Preface to *The Nigger of the "Narcissus,"* p. xi.
9. Zdzislaw Nadjer, *Joseph Conrad: A Chronicle* (New Brunswick: Rutgers Univ. Press, 1983), chs. xi–xii.

I: LORD JIM: Irony and Dream

1. Guerard, p. 176.
2. See Daniel R. Schwartz, *Conrad: Almayer's Folly to Under Western Eyes* (Ithaca: Cornell Univ. Press, 1980), p. 83.
3. Ford Madox Ford, *The Good Soldier* (New York: Knopf, 1951), p. 7.
4. Ibid., p. 5.
5. Peter J. Glassman, *Language and Being: Joseph Conrad and the Literature of Personality* (New York: Columbia Univ. Press, 1976), p. 254.
6. See Royal Roussel, *The Metaphysics of Darkness* (Baltimore: Johns Hopkins Univ. Press, 1971).
7. Schwartz, p. 77.
8. See E. R. Dodds, *The Greeks and the Irrational* (Berkeley and Los Angeles: Univ. of California Press, 1956), ch. 2.
9. J. Hillis Miller, *Fiction and Repetition* (Cambridge: Harvard Univ. Press, 1982), p. 31.
10. Schwartz, p. 83.
11. Guerard, p. 157.
12. David Thorburn, *Conrad's Romanticism* (New Haven: Yale Univ. Press, 1974). See also Ian Watt's extended discussion of Stein, pp. 323–31.

13. Honoré de Balzac, *Père Goriot*, trans. Henry Reed (New York: Signet Classics, 1962), p. 216.
14. Nathaniel Hawthorne, *The Marble Faun* (Boston: Houghton, Mifflin, 1892), [Preface], p. 15.
15. Guerard, p. 162. See also Miller's comments on light and dark in Patusan, p. 38.
16. Tzvetan Todorov, *The Fantastic*, trans. Richard Howard (Cleveland: Press of Western Reserve Univ., 1973), pp. 25, 31.
17. H. and H. A. Frankfort, "The Emancipation of Thought from Myth," in H. and H. A. Frankfort, eds., *Before Philosophy* (Baltimore: Penguin Books, 1949), p. 240.
18. Gérard Genette, *Narrative Discourse*, trans. Jane E. Lewin (Ithaca: Cornell Univ. Press, 1980), p. 232.
19. Guerard, p. 149.
20. Schwartz, p. 82.
21. Charles Dickens, *Little Dorrit* (London: Oxford Univ. Press, 1953), p. 127 (ch. 11).

II: NOSTROMO: The Irony of Faithful Service

1. Edward W. Said, *Beginnings* (New York: Basic Books, 1975), p. 129.
2. Schwartz, p. 143.
3. Quoted in Douglas Hewitt, *Conrad—A Reassessment* (Cambridge: Bowes & Bowes, 1952), p. 50.
4. Said, p. 126.
5. Robert Penn Warren, Introduction, Joseph Conrad, *Nostromo* (New York: Modern Library, 1951), p. xxix. Though my reading of Nostromo's character and role differs from Warren's, I am indebted to several of the ideas presented in this splendid essay.
6. Guerard, p. 204.
7. Said, p. 127.
8. Schwartz, p. 143.
9. See Seymour Chatman, *Story and Discourse* (Ithaca: Cornell Univ. Press, 1978), pp. 107–45.
10. Schwartz, p. 144.
11. Several passages from the original text (1904) do not appear in the Kent edition. These are included in the Modern Library edition (cited in note 5); my quotations use the prefix ML followed by the page number.
12. Said, p. 134.
13. See Guerard, p. 199, and Said, pp. 130–32.
14. Guerard, pp. 210, 216.
15. Schwartz, p. 145.

III: THE SECRET AGENT: The Irony of Home Truths

1. D. W. Harding, "Regulated Hatred: An Aspect of the Work of Jane Austen," *Scrutiny* 8 (1940): pp. 346–62.

2. Guerard, p. 222.
3. Schwartz, p. 167.
4. Claire Rosenfield, *Paradise of Snakes* (Chicago: Univ. of Chicago Press, 1967), p. 90.
5. Guerard, p. 228.
6. Schwartz, p. 162.
7. Christopher Cooper, *Conrad and the Human Dilemma* (London: Chatto & Windus, 1970), p. 20.
8. Guerard, p. 225.
9. Preface to *The Nigger of the "Narcissus,"* p. xiv.
10. Cooper, p. 19.
11. Gustave Flaubert, *Madame Bovary*, trans. Francis Steegmuller (New York: Random House, 1957), p. 216.
12. Cooper, p. 49.
13. Both in himself and in his relation to Conrad, the Assistant Commissioner has been much discussed. For example, Schwartz, rejecting Avrom Fleishman's view of the official as "a moral ideal," argues that the Assistant Commissioner "is mocked by the selfish motives of his quest" to unravel the mystery (Schwartz, p. 163).
14. Guerard, p. 223.
15. Ibid., p. 224.
16. Emile Zola, *Germinal* (Baltimore: Penguin Books, 1954), p. 453. I have emended L. W. Tancock's translation.
17. Schwartz, p. 167.

IV: UNDER WESTERN EYES:
Irony and Women's Strength

1. Schwartz, p. 195.
2. Joseph Conrad, Letter to John Galsworthy (January 6, 1908), quoted in M. D. Zabel, *Craft and Character in Modern Fiction* (New York: Viking Press, 1957), pp. 200–201. Conrad's celebrated phrase "*Cosas de Russia*" has been much discussed. See Guerard, pp. 246–48, and Frank Kermode, *The Art of Telling* (Cambridge: Harvard Univ. Press, 1983), pp. 139–53.
3. Nadjer, p. 373.
4. Ibid., p. 473. "'Slavonism' was evidently synonymous with Dostoevskyism."
5. See for example Cooper, pp. 85–86, and Schwartz, p. 201.
6. Rainer Maria Rilke, *The Notebooks of Malte Laurids Brigge*, trans. M. D. Herter Norton (New York: Capricorn Books, 1958), p. 27.
7. Schwartz, p. 207.
8. Ibid.
9. See Martin Swales, *The Geman Novelle* (Princeton: Princeton Univ. Press, 1977), pp. 21–36, for a discussion of the ramifications of Goethe's seminal remark: "What is a novelle but an unprecedented happening that has actually occurred."
10. Kermode, p. 145.
11. Guerard, p. 245.

12. Schwartz, pp. 196 and 195–211 passim.
13. Kermode, p. 145, refers approvingly to Avrom Fleischman's modernist argument in "Speech and Writing in *Under Western Eyes*," *Conrad: A Commemoration*, ed. Norman Sherry (New York: Barnes & Noble, 1977), pp. 119–28.
14. Zabel, p. 203.
15. Moser, p. 95.
16. Guerard, p. 240.
17. Swales, p. 28.
18. Guerard, p. 247.
19. Moser, p. 96.

Index

Arnold, Matthew, 1
Austen, Jane, 70

Balzac, Honoré de, 22, 28, 94
Beaumarchais, Pierre-Augustin Caron de, 48
Booth, Wayne C., 5
Brontë, Emily, 104

Cervantes, Miguel de, 68–69
Chatman, Seymour, 48n
Childers, Erskine, 84
Conrad, Joseph
    "Gaspar Ruiz," 44
    Heart of Darkness, 1–5, 8–9, 11, 31, 45, 70–71, 102
    Lord Jim, 9–10, 11–12, 16–42, 43, 55–56, 73, 76
    Nigger of the "Narcissus," The, 10, 21, 27, 49, 75
    Nostromo, 8, 12–13, 43–69, 73–74, 82, 120
    Outcast of the Islands, An, 49, 60
    Rescue, The, 47
    Secret Agent, The, 6–7, 10, 13–14, 70–91, 93, 102–3, 118
    Under Western Eyes, 4, 10, 14–15, 42, 80, 91, 92–125
    "Youth," 25–26, 49
Cooper, Christopher, 73, 76, 82, 94
Culler, Jonathan, 5–6

Dickens, Charles, 38, 43, 81
Dodds, E. R., 20

Dostoevsky, Fyodor M., 93–95, 117, 120–21

Eliot, George, 21

Fitzgerald, F. Scott, 19
Flaubert, Gustave, 5–6, 77
Fleishman, Avrom, 85n, 105
Ford, Ford Madox, 17–18, 104
Frankfort, H. and H. A., 34

Genette, Gérard, 36
Gide, André, 8, 19, 27, 95
Glassman, Peter J., 19
Goethe, Johann Wolfgang von, 49
Gogol, Nikolai V., 44
Graham, Cunninghame R. B., 44
Guerard, Albert J.
    on *Heart of Darkness*, 2
    on *Lord Jim*, 16, 20, 23, 37
    on *Nostromo*, 43, 47, 48, 61
    on *The Secret Agent*, 93, 94, 96, 104

Harding, D. W., 70
Hardy, Thomas, 8, 72, 81
Hawthorne, Nathaniel, 28
Hewett, Douglas, 44n

James, Henry, 100
Joyce, James, 27
Jung, C. G., 32

Index

Kafka, Franz, 95
Keats, John, 28
Kermode, Frank, 93, 100, 105
Kleist, Heinrich von, 100

Lawrence, D. H., 8, 106

Mann, Thomas, 8, 27
Miller, J. Hillis, 21, 30n
Morrison, Arthur, 72
Moser, Thomas, 4, 110, 120, 123
Muecke, D. C., 5, 7–8

Nadjer, Zdzislaw, 15, 21, 94n
Novalis, 49

Proust, Marcel, 19

Rilke, Rainer Maria, 95, 106
Rosenfield, Claire, 71
Roussel, Royal, 19

Said, Edward W., 43, 44, 46, 51, 59n

Sarraute, Nathalie, 8
Schiller, Friedrich von, 44
Schwartz, Daniel R.
  on *Lord Jim*, 16, 20, 23, 37
  on *Nostromo*, 43, 47, 48, 61
  on *The Secret Agent*, 71, 72, 85n, 90
  on *Under Western Eyes*, 93, 94, 96, 104
Scott, Sir Walter, 2–3, 21
Swales, Martin, 100n, 117

Thackeray, William Makepeace, 7
Thorburn, David, 27
Todorov, Tzvetan, 31–32
Tolstoy, Leo, 44
Trollope, Anthony, 21
Turgenev, Ivan, 102

Warren, Robert Penn, 45
Watt, Ian, 1, 27n
Watts, Cedric, 2

Zabel, M. D., 93n, 108
Zola, Emile, 72, 81, 84, 90

 is a series of monographs on literature covering the years from 1830 to 1914. Contributions may be critical (historical or theoretical), biographical, bibliographic, comparative, or interdisciplinary.

DANIEL ALBRIGHT, *Tennyson: The Muses' Tug-of-War*

DAVID G. RIEDE: *Matthew Arnold and the Betrayal of Language*

JAMES RICHARDSON, *Vanishing Lives: Style and Self in Tennyson, D. G. Rossetti, Swinburne, and Yeats*

ANTHONY WINNER, *Culture and Irony: Studies in Joseph Conrad's Major Novels*

www.ingramcontent.com/pod-product-compliance
Lightning Source LLC
Chambersburg PA
CBHW011746220426
43667CB00019B/2919